The Jesus Difference

HERBERT EDGAR DOUGLASS

Books by Herbert Edgar Douglass

If I Had One Sermon to Preach (anthology)

Why I Joined

What Ellen White Has Meant to Me (anthology)

We Found This Truth

Perfection: The Impossible Possibility (co-author)

Why Jesus Waits

Jesus—The Benchmark of Humanity (co-author)

Faith, Saying Yes to God

Parable of the Hurricane

The End

How to Survive the 80s (co-author)

Rediscovering Joy (Philippians and Corinthians)

Messenger of the Lord (college/seminary textbook)

How to Survive in the 21st Century

Should We Ever Say, "I Am Saved"?

God at Risk

Feast Days

They Were There (stories of EGW's visions and the people affected)

Truth Matters (an evaluation of Rick Warren's Purpose-Driven Ministry)

Never Been This Late Before

Dramatic Events Predicted by Ellen White

Love Finds a Way (a devotional)

A Fork in the Road

The
Jesus
Difference

HERBERT EDGAR DOUGLASS

Published by Amazing Facts
P.O. Box 1058
Roseville, CA 95678
800-538-7275

Editing by Ken McFarland
Cover design by Matthew Moores
Page design by Page One Communications

Unless otherwise indicated, all Scripture quotations are from the New King James Version of the Bible, copyright © 1979, 1980, 1982, Thomas Nelson, Inc., Publishers.

Library of Congress Cataloging-in-Publication Data

Douglass, Herbert Edgar, 1927-
  The Jesus difference / by Herbert Edgar Douglass.
    p. cm.
  ISBN 978-1-58019-220-0 (alk. paper)
  1. Jesus Christ--Person and offices. I. Title.

  BT203.D68 2008
  232'.8--dc22
                        2008009035

ISBN: 978-1-58019-220-0

Contents

The Author's Invitation

I have written numerous books and articles during the past sixty-one years. Each one has been asked for by somebody, either in the pew or in the publishing world. In other words, someone, somewhere, wanted something more clearly explained.

But this volume has been different. *The Jesus Difference* has always been in the back of my mind, like a hovering shadow or a whispering echo. It seems that each chapter was being framed because I was living "that frame."

Enough years have gone by, and I sense more clearly than ever that most everyone I know has been living out these same chapters in their own personal experiences. Not everyone, however, discovered *The Jesus Difference*. Sometimes, it took me more time than I could wish to also discover *The Jesus Difference*.

So, through the years, the more I pondered each chapter, the more I understood how nigh Jesus comes to all of us! Not a ten-foot-tall Superman! Not a Heavenly Astronaut safely within His spacesuit to avoid the weaknesses and liabilities of humanity! But rather, One willing to "meet life's peril in common with every human soul . . . at the risk of failure and eternal loss."

Once that truth, like a laser beam, enlightened my mind, my whole life was changed. It took away my excuses. It opened up a whole new way of getting out of bed and facing whatever the day would throw at me. It was *The Jesus Difference!*

I resonate with John Bunyan when he finished his "Apology" for writing his awesome *The Pilgrim's Progress:* "O thou come hither, and lay my book, thy head, and heart together."

Herbert Edgar Douglass
Lincoln Hills, California
February 14, 2008

Dedication

To our closest fellow travelers on the Road to Forever:
Jan, Herb, Reatha, Randy, Vivienne Sue, Donna, Chip, and Judy

What Readers Are Saying

Not often do I read a book that truly warms my heart. But this one has done exactly that. At the very beginning it focused my attention on the "same Jesus" that the disciples had known—the attractive, powerful Man who shared totally the human experience, the Man who talked and prayed with the disciples for three years, the Man who experienced with them the storms on Lake Galilee, the Man who performed miracles to feed hungry thousands of people, the Man who raised the dead, the Man whose character radiated love so strongly that even children were drawn to Him. This is the Jesus whom the angels said would "return in like manner."

But what is He doing now? Sad to say, many people do not know, and many others have forgotten. But "the intercession of Christ in man's behalf in the sanctuary above is as essential to the plan of salvation as was His death upon the cross" (*The Great Controversy*, p. 489). This book, then, focuses on "this same Jesus," who, as our Mediator, is seeking to make effectual in our lives the result of His great sacrifice. I believe that all who read this book thoughtfully will have a more personal relationship with Jesus and will see clearly that His ministry in heaven has eternal relevance to every aspect of our lives as we await His return.

—Kenneth H. Wood, former Editor, *Adventist Review*, and
Chairman, Ellen G. White Estate

Dr. Herb Douglass has been my career mentor—and a personal counselor too—from the days when I worked as a 20-something assistant editor on *Insight* magazine on the second floor of the old Review and Herald Publishing Association in Takoma Park, Maryland—and he served as associate editor of the *Adventist Review* one floor up.

A few years later, as incoming book editor at Pacific Press in Mountain View, California, he called me to join him as an associate book editor. I kept wandering off to pastor churches, but again in a few more years, as editorial vice president at Pacific Press, now in Idaho, he called me back to be his book acquisitions editor.

I've learned more from Herb than I can possibly tell: of writing and editing, of theology, of how to live as a man and a Christian in this world. In recent years, it's been my privilege to edit a number of books from his prolific computer. They've all been extraordinary, but this one has lifted my eyes toward the Jesus we both serve as have few books I've ever read. It's deeply personal and practical, it's full of hope, and it reveals the amazing difference Jesus stands ready to make in your life and mine. Buy it. Read it. Then be glad you did!

—Ken McFarland, Editor and Author—and Owner,
Page One Communications

Dr. Douglass has repackaged truth in fresh and sometimes provocative prose. One example: "Joy in hanging at the heat of the day on cruel Calvary?" This question provides entrée into what true seeking of happiness really means. Not only will the reader enjoy the excellent vignettes/illustrations but will also be heartened by the appeal to personal application in practical terms. Underlying it all is the reason for the very existence of the Adventist faith.

—Dale Martin, Ministry Partner Representative
Amazing Facts Ministries

Foreword

Over the years I have helped develop scores of evangelistic handbills.

In the process I have learned there are some central things people want to know before they choose to come to the meetings. It is crucial to answer the most important questions as clearly and simply as possible, such as, "What is it?" "Why is it?" "Where is it?" "When is it?" "Who is the speaker?" or "How can I attend?"

For the handbill to be successful these questions must stand out in the printed handbill copy and be attractively illustrated.

My friend Herb Douglass has done a masterful job of creating an attractive "handbill" beautifully advertising our Savior. *The Jesus Difference* addresses the most important questions about the most important Person who has ever lived.

Who is He? Where is He? Why is He there? What is He doing? How can He be like us? And most important, how can we be like Him?

In his winsome and disarming way, Dr. Douglass gathers some of the most volatile and profound theological issues—then kneads and bakes the manna into angel food everyone can digest. I recommend that everyone take up this book with prayer and a good appetite.

—Doug Batchelor, President and Speaker
Amazing Facts Ministries

"The humanity of the Son of God is everything to us. It is the golden chain that binds our souls to Christ, and through Christ to God. This is to be our study. Christ was a real man; . . .We should come to this study with the humility of a learner, with a contrite heart. And the study of the incarnation of Christ is a fruitful field, which will repay the searcher who digs deep for hidden truth."—*Selected Messages,* bk. 1, p. 244.

ONE

Where Is Jesus Now?

The morning breeze cooled their faces. Jerusalem's dogs were awakening, and street merchants were rolling out their carts. The eleven were walking a familiar path with their resurrected Lord, out of the city and toward their favorite quiet place.

They crossed the Brook Kedron and approached Gethsemane, where Jesus reviewed the awesome instruction He had given them before His lonely night of great agony under the covering olive trees. They listened again to all that precious counsel of vine and branches, of the Holy Spirit, which they yet did not fully understand—of their new relationship with their Heavenly Father, of their new job description—to be to the world what Jesus had been, to glorify their Heavenly Father.

What a journey! For forty days Jesus had been meeting them on several occasions—we know not how many. But they sensed that this morning walk seemed different. Their Lord was intense—His words seemed especially deliberate. He watched their faces to see if His loyal disciples understood each word.

The sun met them as they crested Olivet. Its first rays were reflected off the Temple's towers behind them. Its priests and worshippers were oblivious to the empty meaninglessness of their daily rituals. The Lord of their rituals, spurned and crucified, was soon to leave their beautiful city— never again would they hear His calm, gracious, winsome messages.

Suddenly, the Master Teacher ended His summary of those principles that mattered most. The moment must have been electric. What must His young, 33-year-old face looked like as He gazed at His faithful eleven! They found it hard to breathe, as they sensed that something very special was happening. They knew He had talked about leaving them. But now it seemed, they had so much more to ask Him.

His Ascension

But as their eyes never left His face, He began to ascend. He threw out His hands and with bell-like tones, said, "Fear not. I will never forsake you; I am with you always, even unto the end of the world. Wait for the Holy Spirit whom I have promised; He will be your Power wherever you go" (Matthew 28:20; Acts 1:8).

Could mortal men ever have witnessed a more awesome moment? They eagerly turned back to that cruel city with a fresh perspective—they had a great story to tell, and they had heavenly Power to help them tell it!

But before they turned back to Jerusalem, "two men stood by them in white apparel" with these astounding words: "Men of Galilee, why do you stand gazing up into heaven? This same Jesus, who was taken up from you into heaven, will so come in like manner as you saw Him go into heaven" (Acts 1:10, 11).

"This Same Jesus"

"This same Jesus!" This same Jesus who talked and prayed with them for three years! He who had sailed the Sea of Galilee with them, quieted the sea's fury, and fed the many thousands out of a boy's lunch—this same Jesus was now back in heaven after thirty-three years plus nine months away!

This same Jesus—not a phantom, not even as His former self with all of His divine prerogatives! Not as a disembodied spirit! Not with the "form of God" that was His before He came to this world (Philippians 2:6) but as *man*. Forever, He would be the "same Jesus" but now limited to time and space—time without end! Forever bearing on His body the scars of His brutal crucifixion—visible signs of the cost of mankind's salvation. Forever!

But this "same Jesus" would someday return, just as He left earth 2,000 years earlier, visibly, for all on earth to see Him (Revelation 1:7). Not in some "secret" rapture—but with clouds of angels with trumpets and violins!

At the Heart of the Universe

Until that glorious future return, those first disciples now knew they had a Friend at the heart of the universe, united once more with the Eternal Trio. The disciples knew they would never be forgotten! They had lived long enough with Jesus to know that He was very good about keeping His promises!

Several years later, on one of the blackest days in Jewish history, hurled rocks crushed Stephen, because his accusers could not handle the truth about their crucified Messiah (Acts 7). But God was as gracious as ever. He parted the veil between heaven and earth so that Stephen, and others who heard his witness, would never be in doubt where Jesus is now and how close He is to what is happening on earth: "Look, I see the heavens opened, and the Son of Man standing at the right hand of God" (Acts 7:55, 56).

Holding coats of those rock throwers, young Saul saw it all—but through prejudiced eyes. He was more determined than ever to stamp out the followers of the One who rocked the foundations of Jewish religious practice. Just another example of the old saying: "Who lights the fire at the stake? Not those of full faith; but those of lurking doubt!"

And what Saul saw at Stephen's stoning set the stage for the next dramatic moment, when he heard from Stephen's Jesus (Acts 9:3–8). Amazing, but it was one of the most crucial moments in the history of this earth. Stephen's Jesus stopped Saul in his tracks on the way to Damascus and changed the history of the western world. So convinced now, so persuaded that he had it all wrong and that Stephen had it all right, Saul soon became the most powerful expositor of Christianity in the first century—and maybe for all centuries since. The Lord recognized his acceptance of truth and his integrity by changing his name from Saul to Paul—the Apostle Paul.

Later in one of his epistles, Paul wrote about where Jesus was and still is. He spoke eloquently of Jesus as mankind's High Priest in the heavenly sanctuary (Hebrews 2:17; 3:1; 4:14–16; 5:5; 7:25; 8:1–6; 9:11–14, 24–28; 12: 2, 8). Never a question in Paul's mind where Jesus was—still alive to hear his prayers!

Several years later, at the end of the first century, aged John, on harsh, rocky Patmos, was given an awesome glimpse of his beloved Master. Wasn't that a gracious gesture on our Lord's part—to give His old friend, who had witnessed gloriously to His cause, the final assurance that all was not in vain? John shared with us: "When I saw Him, I fell at his feet as dead. But He laid His right hand upon me, saying to me, 'Do not be afraid; I am the First and the Last. I am He who lives, and was dead, and behold I am alive for evermore, and I have the keys of Hades and of Death'" (Revelation 1:17, 18).

Something Curious and Sad

But as time went on, something very curious and sad happened to the Christian church. Professed Christians lost sight of where Jesus *now* is and what He is *now* doing on our behalf. Through the centuries many in the church fixed their attention on Him dying on the Cross—the personification of human tragedy. They have exalted Jesus as the greatest teacher of righteousness mankind has ever heard, honored him for untainted integrity in full blossom, revered Him for the moral impulse He has injected into human history. They are moved by the utter abandonment to His ideals that drove Him to the Cross rather than flinch or concede to evil. But that is where they last see Him—on the Cross.

Other Christians went further; they fixed their attention on Jesus as the resurrected Savior. They saw Him mingle with His followers for forty days and then marvelously ascend to heaven. But somehow they lost Him in the vagueness of light-years and theological jargon regarding the "atonement" and what His mission really was. Although they know He is at "the right of God" they have had no clear-cut understanding of Christ's continuing role in the working out of the plan of salvation—a role as High Priest that is as essential to salvation as His death on Calvary.

Seeing the gospel only in part

To see Him only on the Cross without a clear understanding of what He is doing today in the heavenly sanctuary is seeing the gospel in part only. To see Him only as the resurrected Lord is also seeing Him only in part. Appealing and winsome is this beautiful picture of love unlimited—God paying the price for a fallen race and rising triumphantly from the grave—a dual demonstration of love and power! But even this beautiful picture has led many to only a partial picture and leads to important misunderstandings, such as believing that His love is irresistible and that someday in God's good time all men and women will be convinced and thus won back to a reunited kingdom of grace and love.

Or, that simple gratefulness in declaring Jesus as Lord and recognizing that He died for everyone's sin automatically ensures that one is "saved" and has a passport for God's new earth.

But the Lord's role in the plan of salvation includes far more than to see Him only on the Cross, wonderful and indispensable as His death was. Or even to see Him as our resurrected Lord, glorious as this truth surely is. In order to understand why Jesus came to this earth in the first place and why He gave us the gospel, in His own words and in the words of His prophets, we must follow Him into the heavenly sanctuary, where Stephen, Paul, and John saw Him—the great High Priest of the human family, the living hope of everyone who seeks pardon and victory over the forces of sin in our lives today.

Throughout the book of Hebrews Paul sings the glorious song of our Lord's continuing ministry for fallen men and women. For example: "Seeing then we have a great High Priest who has passed through the heavens, Jesus, the Son of God, let us hold fast our confession" (Hebrews 4:14).

Something significant

Something very significant to the plan of salvation is going on in heaven today because Jesus is our High Priest. Something significant and special should be going on in the lives of His followers on earth because of Jesus' role as our High Priest.

Following Jesus into the heavenly sanctuary does not depreciate the Cross. God forbid! Without the Cross, no High Priest would be in the heavenly sanctuary today. But what He is doing today is probably the most important subject to be understood by those on Planet Earth. An insightful biblical expositor wrote: "The intercession of Christ in man's behalf in the sanctuary above is as essential to the plan of salvation as was His death upon the Cross."[1]

No wonder Paul urged his readers: "For we do not have a High Priest who cannot sympathize with our weaknesses, but was all things tempted as we are, yet without sin. Let us therefore come boldly to the throne of grace, that we may obtain mercy [pardon] and find grace [power] to help in time of need" (Hebrews 4:15, 16).

In our next chapter, we will look long and carefully at the kind of human being the angels see when they look at our Lord Jesus Christ in the heavenly sanctuary. The angels told the disciples it would be the "same Jesus" with whom they were well-acquainted. Amazing, yet true! Stephen, Paul, and John saw Him—the "same Jesus."

---

1. Ellen G. White, *The Great Controversy* (Nampa, ID: Pacific Press Publishing Association, 1948), 489.

TWO

What Does Jesus Do As Our High Priest?

W hy do we say that understanding the sanctuary truths, especially our Lord's job description as our High Priest, is probably the most important subject that everyone should grasp in these end-times?

We have been told that "the subject of the sanctuary and the investigative judgment should be clearly understood by the people of God." Apparently, this knowledge is to be more than a textbook understanding. Without it the church member will eventually lose his or her soul: "All need a knowledge for themselves of that position and work of their great High Priest. Otherwise it will be impossible for them to exercise the position which God designs them to fill."[1] Ellen White has given such a dire warning about no other biblical subject!

Why is Ellen White so emphatic? What is there about Jesus as our High Priest that is so fundamental to a correct understanding of the mission and message of the Seventh-day Adventist Church and to the spiritual well-being of its members? Furthermore, why is there such a silence in the Christian church generally and some Adventist pulpits in particular, regarding this important biblical doctrine? And why such a strange boredom among many Adventists regarding the sanctuary truths, if they are so vital to the spiritual health of each church member—especially since 1844?

---

1. White, *The Great Controversy,* 488.

The answers are simple: Satan does not want the towering truths about Jesus as our High Priest to be understood! He doesn't mind if church members pay their tithe, recognize the Sabbath as God's holy day, and build larger schools and hospitals. He is not too troubled if church members pray daily for Jesus to forgive their sins and for Him to return soon to this earth. After all, people who did similarly once crucified Jesus!

What Satan hates

But Satan does hate "the great truths that bring to view an atoning sacrifice and an all-powerful mediator. He knows that with him everything depends on diverting minds from Jesus and His truth."[2] He does this by "invent[ing] unnumbered schemes to occupy our minds, that they may not dwell upon the very work with which we ought to be best acquainted."[3]

In other words, if Satan can cause confusion or boredom with two central truths in the plan of salvation—the twin truths of the gospel—he cares not how much else we may know or do. These central truths are 1) the "atoning sacrifice" and 2) the "all-powerful mediator. These twin truths link indissolubly what Jesus has done *for* us and what He wants to do *in* us.[4]

Unlinking these twin truths has been the major, perennial problem in Christianity since apostolic days. Men and women tend to focus on either what Jesus has done *for us* or what He wants to do *in us.* Rarely are these two concepts held in proper relationship as two foci in an ellipse.[5] We call it the "ellipse of truth."

---

2. *Ibid.*

3. *Ibid.*

4. "Our only ground of hope is in the righteousness of Christ imputed to us, and in that wrought by His Spirit working in and through us." White, *Steps to Christ*, 63.

5. A circle has one focus (center); an ellipse has two focuses (foci). In an ellipse, if the two foci separate from each other, we get eventually something like a hotdog! If they get too close to each other we have made a circle. Either way, we no longer have a true ellipse; machines that use the ellipse principle would suddenly not work if the two foci were moved either closer or farther away. A real ellipse needs both foci to function with equal emphasis on each—or it ceases to be an ellipse. For example: if we want a glass of water, we don't ask for hydrogen—or for oxygen. To get water, we must create H20; that is, both hydrogen and oxygen are needed in the water ellipse. We can't have one without the other!

   Theological truths always use the elliptical pattern; for example, God is one focus of the ellipse, and man is the other. In a way, as far as we are concerned, we can't have one without the other. For example, the ellipse of salvation needs grace and faith; if we want salvation, we can't have grace without faith—and vice versa. The ellipse of the gospel can be expressed by joining pardon and power; pardon—without power to

When the atoning sacrifice, what Jesus has done *for us,* is featured disproportionately, too often the record shows that the work of the Holy Spirit is slighted; a cold, rigid, doctrine-oriented religion often develops. Often, in reaction to this overemphasis, equally earnest Christians, who sense the void in their personal experience caused by an overly intellectualized religion, overstress the work of the Holy Spirit or the security of feeling.

But unduly emphasizing what Christ does *in us* focuses disproportionate attention on a person's religious experience and subjective feelings. In so doing, the historic Word and the objective atonement of our Lord are not properly emphasized and are thus obscured. Faith becomes more a matter of feeling and a reflection of a person's religious experience than an obedient response to God, our Creator and Redeemer.

Fundamental connection

What happens when biblical students grasp this fundamental connection to what Jesus has done *for us* and what He wants to do *in us*? We are rescued from the twin errors of overconfident intellectual security on one hand, and overconfident emotionalism, on the other.

To summarize all this in a few words: we must give equal weight to our Lord's merciful pardon and to His merciful power through the Holy Spirit to overcome our sinful patterns. The angel said it best: "You shall call His name Jesus, for He will save his people *from* their sins" (Matthew 1:21, emphasis supplied).

What Satan fears most

What Satan fears most is that some generation will take God seriously and listen to Him carefully. Satan fears that last-day Christians will take God at His word and cooperate with Him in the eradication of sinful habits and thus become indeed faithful witnesses to the power of the gospel (Matthew 24:14). Satan fears that God's loyalists will join their concern for commandment keeping with the "faith of Jesus." (Revelation 14:12). Satan fears that those who reflect the character of Jesus though faith in God's abiding power will prove him wrong before the observing universe.

Satan fears that once fettered men and women, each with a past record of selfishness and spiritual failure, will demonstrate that God's way of life

---

overcome the sin for which we want pardon—is only a partial gospel and thus is not what God intended. When we want to understand Christ's role in our salvation, we note that He is both our Substitute and our Example—we don't have one without the other. When we want to understand Christ's work as our Savior, we see Him on the Cross, and we see Him as our High Priest—we don't have one without the other.

is the happiest, nicest, healthiest way to live. Satan fears that the winsome, appealing character of these commandment keepers will hasten the Advent of Jesus and his own final destruction.

Satan fears that these glorious possibilities will be uncovered when men and women study what Jesus is doing now in the heavenly sanctuary. He knows better than many professed Christians that linking God's gifts of pardon and power would spell his doom—and he wants to hang on to life as long as possible—forever, if has anything to do about it!

Sanctuary makes everything clearer

All of which brings us back to Jesus in the heavenly sanctuary, where all these truths are made clearer. The longer all heaven and unfallen intelligences throughout the universe take a look at the "same Jesus" who left this earth 2,000 years ago, the louder they sing about God's wisdom and trustworthiness.

What do they see? Not the same Jesus who once was their great Leader, a member of the Heavenly Trio from the time they were created! But they do see that "same Jesus" who walked the hills of Palestine, a member of the human race forever, just like Enoch, Moses, Elijah, and the others resurrected when He was (Matthew 27:52).

What great truth do they now understand beyond a doubt? They see a Man who faced Satan on his home court, who "had to be made like his brethren in every respect, so that he might become a merciful and faithful high priest" (Hebrew 2:17, RSV). They see a Man who conquered every temptation to serve Himself, proving that all men and women, with the same power available to them that He had, can live a victorious life (Revelation 3:20). Our Lord's thirty-three years of perfect obedience to His Father's will, fighting "the battle as every child of humanity must fight it,"[6] silences every one of Satan's accusation regarding God's unfairness in making laws that could not be kept by truly free moral agents.

Jesus is the answer to any possible question that could arise in any far-off unfallen world as to whether God could be trusted or not. Unfallen angels and unfallen created intelligences were once troubled by Satan's insinuations that God was not fair to make laws that would curb the yearn for freedom. They heard Satan accuse God of first-class selfishness—of wanting everyone else to be self-denying, but not Himself.

Now there He is—the Victor in the heaviest, most furious attacks that the mean, evil mind of Satan could devise from the moment of Jesus' birth

---

6. White, *The Desire of Ages*, 49.

to His last gasp on the Cross. No wonder the angels sing as never before! Satan is the liar, and God can be trusted—sin does have consequences, and Jesus showed the ultimate in self-denial. When they see their resurrected Lord, they raise their voices an octave—"Satan is a liar, and God can be trusted—Satan is a liar, and God can be trusted!"

How did John "hear" it? Listen: "Great and marvelous are Your works, Lord God Almighty! Just and true are Your ways" (Revelation 15:3).

But what do we see?

Now, what do *we* see when *we* gaze at "this same Jesus" in the heavenly sanctuary? Ah, He becomes the living answer to every human problem on this sin-swept planet. We also see Him as our Worthy Lord but from a different angle than the unfallen universe. We see our Lord as the only answer to two core questions that have plagued all men and women from the Garden of Eden to our day: how can we deal with crushing guilt—and how can we safely face Satan's "fiery darts" (Ephesians 6:16), those appeals, enticements, to live life our way instead of honoring our Lord whom we profess to serve?

Ellipse of Truth

Ah, the ellipse of truth! On one hand, we see our "sacrificial atonement"; on the other, we see our "all-powerful Mediator"–exactly what we need, hour by hour. He died the death of Gethsemane and Calvary so that none of us need die for our sins. He paid the cost of our freedom. He proved Satan a liar when he said that Eve could disobey God and not die (Genesis 3:4). For die He did—the spotless Son of man. Thus, He proved that God is fair and just—sin does have terrible consequences, and our Lord's life and death proved all that. His loyal followers may sleep for a while in the graves of earth, but they need never really die!

Our Lord's scars will forever remind everyone that sin costs. It was an awful way to settle the issue, but Jesus paid the cost for you and me. We will never get what we deserve because of Him, now on the throne at the heart of the universe. I am more aware of this mighty gift the longer I live. We live on the wings of forgiveness—theologians call it *justification*—our "title" to our home in the new earth.

But we also see Him as our "all-powerful Mediator." This thought also gets deeper and higher the longer I live. It is one thing to take a deep breath every time we sing of our Lord's

"Amazing grace! How sweet the sound, that saved a wretch like me."

It is equally precious to sing,

"Through many dangers, toils, and snares, I have already come; 'Tis grace hath brought me safe thus far, and grace will lead me home."

The "grace [that] will lead me home" is the grace, the power, of God, promised by Jesus, our "great high priest who has passed through the heavens. . . . Let us therefore come boldly to the throne of grace, that we may obtain mercy and find grace to help in time of need" (Hebrews 4:14–16). Theologians call this magnificent divine-human co-op plan *sanctification* (God's plan for fitting us to live forever).

The first half of the gospel ellipse

The first half of the ellipse of truth, our Lord's sacrificial atonement, has been more generally understood by the Christian church than has His high-priestly mediation. In fact, the fuller understanding of our Lord's work as Mediator (1 Timothy 2:5) has been the distinctive contribution of Seventh-day Adventists.

Remember: Satan is not displeased if church members emphasize the sacrificial atonement in sermons and songs, if the benefits of what Christ has done *for* us are not joined with what Christ wants to do, through the Holy Spirit, "in and through us."[7]

Therefore, we should look carefully at our Lord's intercessory, mediatorial role as our High Priest. His priesthood is the only link any human being has between God and man—the "one mediator between God and men, the man Christ Jesus" (1 Timothy 2:5). When He entered the heavenly sanctuary at His ascension, He "entered by His own blood, to shed upon His disciples the benefits of His atonement."[8]

Other half of gospel ellipse

One of those benefits was the other half of the gospel ellipse—the work of the Holy Spirit. The Holy Spirit "as a regenerating agent" completes Christ's saving work, and "without this the sacrifice of Christ would have been of no avail."[9] The Holy Spirit "makes effectual what has been wrought out by the world's Redeemer."[10]

To put it another way, "The intercession of Christ in man's behalf in the

---

7. White, *Steps to Christ*, 63.

8. White, *Early Writings*, 260.

9. White, *The Desire of Ages*, 671.

10. *Ibid.*

sanctuary above is as essential to the plan of salvation as was His death upon the cross."[11]

Where has deep theology been said any clearer? A perfect example of the ellipse of truth!

Let's think for a moment about two specific roles Christ's High-priestly ministry fulfills as our "all-powerful Mediator":

1) He silences the accusations of Satan "with arguments founded not upon our merits, but on His own."[12] His perfect life of obedience, sealed by a death that wrung the heart of God and exposed the awfulness and the terrible end of sin became the basis for the reconciliation between man and God. *He earned the right to forgive us.*[13]

2) He is free to provide the power of grace to all those who choose to live overcoming lives: "He is the High Priest of the church, and He has a work to do which no other can perform. By His grace He is able to keep every man from transgression."[14]

Significance of Christ's intercessory, mediatorial work

Seen in the light of the cosmic controversy between good and evil, between the central figures, Christ and Satan, our Lord's intercessory, mediatorial work takes on great significance. When Satan says that sinful men and women do not deserve forgiveness, that they are not entitled to eternal life any more than he is, that God has asked too much from created beings and is therefore unreasonable and unfair—Jesus stands up in full view of watching worlds as the eternal answer to these questions.

What do angels and unfallen worlds "see"? They see "this same Jesus" that men and women saw 2,000 years ago! They see a Man who was born as all children are born, now grown to adulthood. They see a Man who had all the liabilities of humanity but who went nose-to-nose with Satan—and never flinched. He shut Satan's lying mouth. He earned the right to be our Saviour and High Priest!

With the right to forgive us, Jesus also earned the right to intercede in the lives of His loyal followers. He breaks through the power with which Satan has held them captive. He helps to develop within His followers

---

11. White, *The Great Controversy,* 489.

12. White, *Testimonies,* vol. 5 (Nampa: Pacific Press Publishing Association, 1882), 472.

13. White, *The Desire of Ages,* 745.

14. White, *Signs of the Times,* February 14, 1900.

a strengthened will to resist sinful tendencies. It is the same defense by which He Himself conquered sin.

Christ's intercessions

This kind of intercessory mediation, we need daily until Jesus returns:

> "Everyone who will break from the slavery and service of Satan, and will stand under the blood-stained banner of Prince Immanuel will be kept by Christ's intercessions. Christ, as our Mediator, at the right hand of the Father, ever keeps us in view, for it is as necessary that He should keep us by His intercessions as that He should redeem us with His blood. If He lets go His hold of us for one moment, Satan stands ready to destroy. Those purchased by His blood, He now keeps by His intercession."[15]

His "purchase" and His "keeping power" is another way of describing Jesus as our "atoning Sacrifice" and "all-powerful Mediator." In this salvation ellipse, Jesus spotlights how God plans to eradicate sin from the universe. This is not done by "declaring" it eradicated, or by sponging clean everyone's record with a mighty sweep of mercy. If this were so, the wisdom and justice of God Himself would be forever suspect; nothing would have been settled in the great controversy as to whether God was fair in setting laws that no one could keep—or whether He was just in irrevocably casting from heaven Satan and one third of the angels (see Revelation 12:3,4).

The only way for sin to be destroyed while preserving both the sinner and God's justice is for the rebel to become a loyal son or daughter, willingly and habitually. Sin is a created being's clenched fist in the face of his Creator; sin is the creature, distrusting God, deposing Him as the Lord of his life. The consequences of such rebellion are deadly, as the history of this dreary world reveals.

The one thing God cannot overlook is sham. He doesn't play word-games. Nothing is settled if church members claim the name of Christ but not His power; or claim His power but not His character. This is the truth that makes Satan tremble!

Satan is mightily disturbed, actually furious (Revelation 12:17), when he sees men and women actually reflecting the gracious appeal of "the same Jesus" whom He has hated since the war in heaven (Revelation 12:7).

No wonder Satan is delighted when the sanctuary truths are mystified, obscured, or set aside as a boring subject. No wonder Ellen White spoke

---

15. Ellen G. White comments on Romans 8:34, *The Seventh-day Adventist Commentary,* vol. 6, 1078. Notice the ellipse of truth.

plainly: "All need to become more intelligent in regard to the work of the atonement, which is going on in the sanctuary above. When this grand truth is seen and understood those who hold it will work in harmony with Christ to prepare a people to stand in the great day of God, and their efforts will be successful."[16]

---

16. *Testimonies,* vol. 5, 575.

THREE

What Kind of "Man" Is Our High Priest?

The two angels told the eleven disciples that they would see "the same Jesus" when He returned (Acts 1:11). The unfallen angels received Jesus back but not as their Lord "looked" when He left heaven over thirty years earlier to come to earth. They see Him now as "the same Jesus" the disciples knew.

What kind of a human being was Jesus? This question is one of the most important questions that can be asked—it lies at the heart of man's salvation and at the center of the Great Controversy between God and Satan.

Paul wrote clearly

Paul obviously had the facts straight regarding how human Jesus had come to be here, when He was a baby boy in Bethlehem. Paul used language that the average person could understand. When church members in Rome, Colosse, or Corinth read Paul's letters, no one needed a theologian or a Greek teacher to explain what he was writing. To the Romans, Jesus "was born of the seed of David, according to the flesh" (Rom. 1:3). In fact, Jesus came in the "likeness [not the unlikeness] of sinful flesh, on account of sin" (Rom. 8:3).[1]

---

1. C. E. B. Cranfield, *The International Critical Commentary, The Epistle to the Romans* (Edinburgh: T & T Clark Limited, 1975), 380–382. Cranfield rejects "the traditional solution," which asserts that Paul "introduced ὁμοίωμα [likeness] in order to avoid implying that the Son of God assumed *fallen* human nature, the sense being: like our fallen flesh,

Who has ever given up so much?

To the Philippians Paul focused on Christ's magnificent cascade of humility (another insight into the character of God) when He became a human being. The first eleven verses of the second chapter give us one of the most glorious sweeps of the plan of salvation. Plumbing their depths, along with similar passages elsewhere, brings forth tears of amazement as well as thankfulness. Where in human history has anyone ever given up so much for so many ungrateful people—all the while, knowing in advance that billions of human beings would reject Him, even murder Him!

Look at Jesus, equal with God—in His divinity (Philippians 3:6). Observe Him as He "emptied himself, taking the form of a servant, being born in the likeness (ὁμοιώματι) [that is, not the "unlikeness"] of men" (verse 7)—His real humanity.

Watch Him grow up as any baby boy must, maturing into a servant-leader—humanity's Example. Contemplate Him on the cross—His sacrificial atonement and humanity's Saviour. Turn your eyes to the future, to His glorious exaltation when "every knee" (verse 10) shall bow before Him—still in

---

because really flesh, but only like, and not identical with it, because unfallen. This . . . is open to the general theological objection that it was not unfallen, but fallen, human nature which needed redeeming. . . .The word ὁμοίωμα does have its sense of 'likeness;' but the intention is not in any way to call in question or to water down the reality of Christ's σὰρξ ἁμαρτίας but to draw attention to the fact that, while the Son of God truly assumed σὰρξ ἁμαρτίας He never became σὰρξ ἁμαρτίας and nothing more, nor even σὰρξ ἁμαρτίας indwelt by the Holy Spirit and nothing more (as a Christian might be described as being), but always Himself." Then Cranfield quotes Barrett approvingly, who understands Paul as thinking that 'Christ took precisely the same fallen nature that we ourselves have' and yet 'remained sinless because he constantly overcame a proclivity to sin.' . . . The difference between Christ's freedom from actual sin and our sinfulness is not a matter of the character of His human nature (of its being not quite the same as ours), but of what He did with His human nature. . . . We . . . understand Paul's thought to be that the Son of God assumed the selfsame fallen human nature that is ours, but that in His case that fallen human nature was never the whole of Him—He never ceased to be the eternal Son of God." H. C. G. Moule, in *The Epistle to the Romans*, p. 211, wrote that Jesus overcame "in our identical nature, under all those conditions of earthly life which for us are sin's vehicles and occasions, . . . making man's earthly conditions the scene of sin's defeat." Karl Barth wrote in his massive *Church Dogmatics*, under the section entitled "Very God and Very Man": "He is a man as we are, . . . equal to us in the state and condition into which our disobedience has brought us. . . . He was not a sinful man. But inwardly and outwardly His situation was that of a sinful man. . . . Freely He entered into solidarity and necessary association with our lost existence. Only in this way 'could' God's revelation to us, our reconciliation with Him, manifestly become an event in Him and by Him. . . . But there must be no weakening or obscuring of the saving truth that the nature, which God assumed in Christ, is identical with our nature as we see it in the light of the Fall. If it were otherwise, how could Christ be really like us? What concern would we have with Him?"

His humanity as our "all-powerful Mediator," forever the answer to all misapprehensions, false charges, and lies about the character of God. The big picture—it's all there in Paul's second chapter to the Philippians.[2]

In writing to the Hebrews, Paul emphasized Christ's divinity as well as His humanity, in order to make clear that the Galilean Jesus was exactly what was needed to prove Satan wrong in the Great Controversy. Paul noted that Jesus was "the express image of God" and, since His ascension, now sits on the "right hand of the Majesty on High" (Heb. 1:3). In chapter two, the apostle emphasized our Lord's humanity by stating categorically that Jesus "likewise shared in the same" humanity that all men and women have.[3] Paul went further: Jesus did not take unto himself the status of angels but took on himself "the seed (sperm—σπερματος) of Abraham" (verse 16).

Straightforward answer

Recognizing that Jesus would be born of the "seed of Abraham," what could this mean? A most insightful author gave us a straightforward answer:

"It would have been an almost infinite humiliation for the Son of God to take man's nature, even when Adam stood in his innocence in Eden. But Jesus accepted humanity when the race had been weakened by four thousand years of sin. Like every child of Adam He accepted the results of the working of the great law of heredity. What these results were is shown in the history of His earthly ancestors. He came with such a heredity to share our sorrows and temptations, and to give us the example of a sinless life.

"Satan in heaven had hated Christ for His position in the courts of God. He hated Him the more when he himself was dethroned. He hated Him who pledged Himself to redeem a race of sinners. Yet into the world where Satan claimed dominion God permitted His Son to come, a helpless babe, subject to the weakness of humanity. He permitted Him to meet life's peril in common with every human soul, to fight the battle as every child of humanity must fight it, at the risk of failure and eternal loss." [4]

---

2. See Herbert E. Douglass, *Rediscovering Joy* (Hagerstown, MD: Review and Herald Publishing Association, 1994), Chapter 5, "Knowing Why Jesus Became Human," 54–63.

3. The "likewise" of Heb. 2:14 can be compared with "likeness" of Romans 8:3 and Philippians 2:7.

4. *The Desire of Ages*, 49. In a telling moment in the video, "Black Hawk Down," during the tragic Battle of the Bakara Market in Mogadishu, Somalia, in October 1993, an Army Ranger colonel is in charge of a small convoy of Humvees trying to return to base amidst heavy gun- and rocket-fire. He stops the convoy, drags a dead driver out of his seat, and barks at a bleeding sergeant standing in shock: "Get into that truck

Paul and Ellen White answered the question as to the kind of "man" Jesus became at birth. He would "fight the battle as every child of humanity must fight it, at the risk of failure and eternal loss."

Or, to put it another way, why did Jesus have to be made like human beings "in all things" (Hebrews 2:17; "in every respect," RSV)? For two reasons: 1) so that He could face Satan as any other human being must face him face-to-face, and prove him a liar! He would "destroy [Gr. "paralyze"] him who had the power of death, that is, the devil" (verse 14) and thus release "those who through fear of death were all their lifetime subject to bondage" (verse 15); 2) so that He might earn the right to become humanity's "merciful and faithful High Priest" (verse 17).[5]

In every sense of the word, He had to become like men and women "in every respect" (not merely "like them" in the sense he was not like a zebra or a dog), so that He could become our High Priest *because* "he was in all points tempted as we are, yet without sin" (Hebrews 4:15).

Paul's thundering logic

Paul's thundering logic is overwhelming! Only after becoming a human being "in every respect (yet, without sin)," could Jesus have genuine empathy and compassion, not mere sympathy, when He became our High Priest "since he himself is also beset by weakness" (Hebrew 5:2).[6]

What kind of human experience did our Lord share with us? First of all, prayer was a necessity: "In the days of His flesh, . . He had offered up prayers and supplications, with vehement cries and tears to Him who was able to save Him from death." Jesus did not have an easy life, somehow living above the common, normal struggles of all men and women. He needed the grace (inflowing power) of God to endure loneliness, bitter hostility, and misunderstanding—as we all do. And His prayer life was not always sweet exchanges; prayers were wrenched from His mouth with "cries and tears" (verse 7).

---

and drive." The sergeant replies, "But, I'm shot, Colonel." Colonel's reply: "Everybody's shot—get in and drive." Jesus came down into the worst firefight in history. But He was no bystander. He too was shot, like everyone else. With that kind of experience, He surely knows how to encourage the rest of us—because we all have been shot!

5. On Calvary, "Jesus was earning the right to become the advocate of men in the Father's presence."—*The Desire of Ages*, 745.

6. "He put off His crown, and divested Himself of His royal robe, to take upon Him human nature, that humanity might touch humanity. As the world's Redeemer, He passed through all the experiences through which we must pass."—*Signs of the Times*, July 12, 1899. "He knows by experience what are the weaknesses of humanity, what are our wants, and where lies the strength of our temptations."—*The Desire of Ages*, 329.

Further, Jesus "learned obedience" (verse 8). He was not born automatically obedient! He did not automatically, spontaneously, respond to all occasions, whether with men or face-to-face with Satan, with a heavenly built-in brain that could never fail, give in, or sin.

On the contrary, Jesus grew as any other child would develop. The powers of his mind and body "developed gradually, in keeping with the laws of childhood."[7] He "gained knowledge as we may do."[8] Day after day, He faced the same "risk of failure" as every child or adult must.[9] As today's teenagers would say, Jesus' life on earth was not a "slam-dunk." He "increased in wisdom and stature, and in favor with God and men" (Luke 2:52), as every other boy or girl could and should.

How to mature

He taught us how to mature, to become "perfected" (Hebrews 5:9) so that Satan could find nothing in Him to throw up triumphantly before the universe (John 14:30), saying that even Jesus couldn't keep God's laws and still be joyful.[10] Jesus nailed Satan at every opportunity!

Everyone has the same road to walk as Jesus: "The positiveness and energy, the solidity and strength of character, manifested in Christ are to be developed in us, through the same discipline that He endured. And the grace that He received is for us."[11]

We have just read a remarkable promise—Jesus needed the grace of God to live the life of faith, even as we do today. In fact, the grace of God provided daily *enabled* Jesus to live the life of faith. And the life of faith kept Jesus from sinning. Such is the description that will identify Christians in the end time (Revelation 14:12).

Philip Yancey saw it well: "When a light is brought into a room, what was a window becomes also a mirror reflecting back the contents of that room. In Jesus not only do we have a window to God, we also have a

---

7. *Ibid.*, 68.

8. *Ibid.*, 70.

9. *Ibid.*, 49.

10. "He had kept His father's commandments, and there was no sin in Him that Satan could use to his advantage. This is the condition in which those must be found who shall stand in the time of trouble. It is in this life that we are to separate sin from us, through faith in the atoning blood of Christ. . . . It rests with us to co-operate with the agencies which Heaven employs in the work of conforming our characters to the divine model."—*The Great Controversy*, 623.

11. *The Desire of Ages*, 73.

mirror of ourselves, a reflection of what God had in mind when he created this 'poor, bare, forked animal.' Human beings were, after all, created in the image of God; Jesus reveals what that image should look like. . . . By enacting what we ought to be like, he showed who we were meant to be and how far we miss the mark."[12]

Summary

"In every respect" (Hebrews 2:17, RSV) Jesus became the benchmark for what men and women are called to be. The divine grace that helped Jesus to become our benchmark is the same grace promised to all men and women of faith.

In the middle of an otherwise unremarkable and deserted road on the Kansas-Nebraska border in north-central Kansas is located the surveyor's benchmark from which all property in Kansas, Nebraska, and parts of South Dakota, Wyoming, and Colorado are referenced. Soon after the passing of the Kansas-Nebraska Act in 1854, a survey was commissioned by the United States government so that the lands newly opened for settlement could be properly and legally plotted out for the homesteaders.

Today, that original surveyor's benchmark—"Red Sandstone Marker," made by Charles Manners in 1856—can be seen under a manhole cover in the middle of that deserted road. In recent times, a brass surveyor's benchmark has been placed on that special stone.

Jesus became that model man, the Example who shut Satan's mouth. His life became the universe's Benchmark, from which all created intelligences can be referenced. Of course, such an exposé of Satan's lies drove Satan to murder Jesus. But in so doing, Jesus fulfilled His other reason for becoming a man—to pay the cost of man's salvation. He forever will be our "atoning sacrifice" and "all-powerful Mediator."

---

12. Philip Yancey, *The Jesus I Never Knew* (Grand Rapids, MI: Zondervan Publishing House, 1995), 269, 270.

FOUR

What Difference Does All This Make to Us Today?

It is one thing to know Jesus as an historical figure. It is one thing to know that He died on the Cross, took our place, and gave us an unforgettable picture of how far God would go to redeem us. It is one thing to know that He is in heaven "at the right hand of the throne of the Majesty in heavens" (Hebrews 8:1).

But it is something else to know that He is the "same Jesus" whom boys and girls followed along Palestinian paths under palm trees, listening to wonderful stories about God. He is the "same Jesus" who settled the doubts of intellectual professors such as Nicodemus. The "same Jesus" who brought hope and joy into homes that had seen their children die. And the same Jesus who patiently worked with sinners who failed Him and themselves, even seven times.

Remember, throughout all these unnumbered human experiences with children and their parents, soldiers, and religious leaders, Jesus was earning the right to be our High Priest.[1] No other way!

Before we examine what that grand thought means for us today, we should look at another question first: How long will Jesus remain a human being? The answer to that is simple—but so profound that we will be

---

1. "Jesus was earning the right to become the advocate of men in the Father's presence." White, *The Desire of Ages,* 745.

thinking through its implications for as long as robins sing and eagles soar.

Human being forever

Whatever God gives with one hand, He does not take away with the other! When God "gave" Jesus to Planet Earth, it was the simple truth that Jesus became part of the human family forever. Forever, and forevermore, He would retain His human nature!

Jesus came to this world and took our human nature, not for thirty-three years, "but to retain his nature in the heavenly courts, an everlasting pledge of the faithfulness of God."[2] Jesus truly "gave" Himself to Planet Earth.

God adopted human nature *forever!* That's why Paul could rejoice that Jesus has gone back to heaven to "become High Priest forever" (Hebrews 6:20). Forever, He will be at the heart of the universe, visibly connecting the whole universe to this struggling rebel Planet Earth. He is vitally connected with the great-controversy struggle going on in each of our lives today. He has been here, and He knows exactly what we need to "overcome. . . as [He] also overcame" (Revelation 3:21).

Jesus, forever at the heart of the universe, now and evermore, will be an eternal reminder of how much freedom costs—how much God was willing to risk in order to have again a safe, secure universe. No one will ever question God's motives again. No one will ever wonder if God Himself practices self-denial or if He can be trusted. Just look at His hands! Those hands will tell us without further words how much He denied Himself, how much His love embraces, how far God went to rescue any one of the redeemed!

All this and more will remind us forever why "The Saviour has bound Himself to humanity by a tie that is never to be broken. . . . To assure us of His immutable counsel of peace, God gave His only-begotten Son to become one of the human family, forever to retain His human nature. . . . God has adopted human nature in the person of His Son, and has carried the same into the highest heaven."[3]

---

2. White, *Selected Messages*, bk. 1, 258.

3. *The Desire of Ages*, 25. "Christ thought it not robbery to be equal with God, and yet He pleased not Himself. He took upon Himself human nature for no other purpose than to place man on vantage ground before the world and the whole heavenly universe. He carries sanctified humanity to heaven, there always to retain humanity as it would have been if man had never violated God's law. The overcomers, who upon the earth were

Imprisoned with His own creation

Contemplate the thought. It staggers the mind. We can understand somewhat the marvel of our Lord's birth in Bethlehem, when He imprisoned Himself within His own creation, within the womb of His mother. But for the Lord of Creation, who walked among the stars and whirled new galaxies into their orbits, to be *forever* cabined within time and space—this stretches our minds across unlimited oceans of love. Something like a Great Inventor who created a machine that would solve all the energy and environmental problems of earth, but it would not work unless He got within it and never again would get out! Jesus locked Himself within human nature forever—just to save you and me!

This thought alone will hold us virtually speechless as long as bluebirds fly in the celestial skies of the New Earth.

Let's now trace how "this same Jesus" relates today to children, to teenagers, to the suffering of others, to others who lost loved ones, to those who doubted, to those who are facing their own death, to those who face the Evil One, to what seems to be a lost cause and to other highly important events in His short but very full life on earth.

Prayer

But first, what does "the same Jesus" want us to know about prayer? What do we learn when we watch Him pray?

▸ As a human, *He had to pray.* Why? Because He said, "I can do nothing on my own authority" (John 5:30). Paul understood this: "In the days of his flesh, when He had offered up prayers and supplications, with vehement cries and tears, to Him who was able to save Him from death, and was heard because of His godly fear" (Hebrews 5:7).

▸ Jesus prayed for Himself as well as for others. Why? Because, as a human, He needed divine help to withstand the Evil One: "As one with us, a sharer in our needs and weaknesses, He was wholly dependent upon God, and in the secret place of prayer He sought divine strength, that He might go forth braced for duty and trial. In a world of sin Jesus endured struggles and torture of soul. In communion

partakers of the divine nature, He makes kings and priests unto God."—Manuscript 156, Oct. 26, 1903, cited in *Upward Look*, 313; "As the Son of God He gives security to God in our behalf, and as the eternal Word, as one equal with the Father, He assures us of the Father's love to usward who believe His pledged word. When God would assure us of His immutable counsel of peace, He gives His only begotten Son to become one of the human family, forever to retain His human nature as a pledge that God will fulfill His word."—White, *Review and Herald*, April 3, 1894.

with God He could unburden the sorrows that were crushing Him. Here He found comfort and joy."[4] Jesus "sought His Father daily for fresh supplies of needed grace . . . [for] power to resist evil and to minister to the needs of men."[5]

▶ Jesus prayed because He needed what we all need daily—"a fresh baptism of the Holy Spirit."[6]

▶ Jesus prayed to God, not only to the Omnipotent One, but also to our Heavenly Father. Calling God "Our Father" was a dramatic announcement. We are not orphans; we have a father's heart beating at the center of the universe! In fact, this was His "favorite theme . . . the paternal tenderness and abundant grace of God."[7] No wonder we can "trust all with God![8]

▶ Because we know all this, we should boldly, as "this same Jesus" would, "accept His plan for your life. As children of God, you will hold His honor, His character, His family, His work, as the objects of your highest interest. It will be your joy to recognize and honor your relation to your Father and to every member of His family."[9]

▶ We will see what "this same Jesus" understood, that prayer does not "work any change in God;" rather, it should "bring us into harmony with God."[10]

▶ We will understand more clearly why Jesus inserted "Hallowed be Thy Name" in His model prayer—it was the core motive in His life: "In every act of life you are to make manifest the name of God. This petition calls upon you to possess His character. You cannot hallow His name; you cannot represent Him to the world, unless in life and character you represent the very life and character of God. This you can do only through the acceptance of the grace and righteousness of Christ."[11]

▶ So—when we pray as Jesus did, "this same Jesus" will respond to you

4. White, *The Desire of Ages*, 362.

5. _____, *Acts of the Apostles*, 56.

6. _____, *Christ's Object Lessons*, 135.

7. Ibid., 40.

8. Ibid., 146.

9. White, *The Mount of Blessing*, 105.

10. _____, *Christ's Object Lessons*, 143.

11. _____, *The Mount of Blessing*, 107.

as His Heavenly Father and Holy Spirit responded to His prayers. Believe it! Live it!

Hard-working Students

Students of all ages are under pressure, both from within and without. Nothing is really learned without stress. That's the price we pay to be worth listening to or to be worth a paycheck. What does "this same Jesus" want all students to know—and know through experience? How did He "increase in wisdom and stature" (Luke 2:52)?

▸ Jesus learned as all boys and girls must learn, from kindergarten to beyond graduate work. He did not come to earth with the brain He had before He became a fetus in Mary's womb. His mind and body developed "in keeping with the laws of childhood. . . . He gained knowledge as we do."[12] Much of His teaching was oral, but His parents, in some way, made the parchments of the Hebrew Old Testament available, though He did not gain His biblical knowledge in the synagogue schools.

▸ The joy and excitement of all this is that "every child may gain knowledge as Jesus did."[13] Through the beauty, grandeur, and complexity of nature, Jesus gained a fresh understanding of what God was like. Through the Holy Scriptures He developed a deeper understanding of God's plan to rescue men and women from the consequences and power of sin. Through daily, prayerful communion with His Heavenly Father, His "mental and moral faculties" were strengthened. Through His work education as He learned the carpenter trade, He learned "exactness and thoroughness. . . . and discipline."[14]

▸ What do we learn about the young life of our Lord that "this same Jesus" can today pass on to us? This is glorious: "The positiveness and energy, the solidity and strength of character, manifested in Christ are to be developed in us, through the same discipline that He endured. And the grace that He received is for us."[15]

▸ What special messages that young Jesus once learned, are the same lessons that "this same Jesus" wants students to know today?

---

12. ____, *The Desire of Ages*, 68, 70.

13. Ibid.

14. Ibid., 72, 73.

15. Ibid., 73.

▸ He doesn't emphasize a consecrated heart above a disciplined, searching head. I like the way Ellen White put it: "The truths of the divine word can be best glorified by those who serve Him intelligently."[16] In other words, humility should never be linked with ignorance.

▸ Notice the clarity of this appeal: "God requires the training of the mental faculties. He designs that His servants shall possess more intelligence and clearer discernment than the worldling, and He is displeased with those who are too careless or too indolent to become efficient, well-informed workers. The Lord bids us love Him with all the heart, and with all the soul, and with all the strength, and with all the mind. This lays upon us the obligation of developing the intellect to its fullest capacity, that with all the mind we may know and love our Creator."[17]

Why am I emphasizing all this? This kind of educational philosophy is what helped Jesus "to increase in wisdom and stature." This is the kind of counsel He wants to give to every weary, struggling, student—no matter how young or old.

Children

When children today think about God, what goes on in their minds? Is He far off, beyond the sky, sitting on a big throne? Is He more like the cop in the rearview mirror? Or like a stern judge?

What did children see when they looked at Jesus? Ah, at least they jumped on His lap! Some slept in His arms while He taught their parents. Some kissed Jesus with grateful affection.[18] No child would do all that with a grumpy man or woman.

There was something attractive about Jesus that made children feel safe. He listened to their stories, their hopes, and their hurts. He blessed them, and they kept coming back!

Have parents and others portrayed "this same Jesus" as young Palestinians knew Him, or have they painted a picture of a stern, unsmiling Jesus that was inspired by the Evil One? Our first task in the home and in the church family is to present Jesus as He really was, so that the young today can picture "this same Jesus" when they want to feel safe and understood by the God of heaven.

16. ____, *Fundamentals of Christian Education*, 45.

17. ____, *Christ's Object Lessons*, 333.

18. ____, *The Desire of Ages*, 592.

Teenagers

Jesus well knew the crosswinds that blow across every teenager's life. Loyalty to parents, the urge to be independent, career issues, and the opposite sex—all this and more is every teenager's challenge. Jesus was no exception.

Further, we know that God did not "rig" our Lord's pathway through His teenage years by sheltering Him from the normal thoughts and temptations that plague any growing boy or girl. Hardly!

Ellen White was frank: "He was subject to all the conflicts which we have to meet, that He might be an example to us in childhood, youth, and manhood."[19] In fact, she made it clear at a time when others had difficulty understanding Jesus as a truly human being: "Christ was a child; he had the experience of a child; he felt the disappointments and trials that children feel; he knew the temptations of children and youth."[20] Further, "Let children bear in mind that the child Jesus had taken upon himself human nature, and was in the likeness of sinful flesh, and was tempted of Satan as all children are tempted."[21]

In writing to her nephew, Frank Belden, in early manhood, Ellen White counseled: "You have not a difficulty that did not press with equal weight upon Him, not a sorrow that His heart has not experienced. . . . Jesus once stood in age just where you now stand. Your circumstances, your cogitations at this period of your life, Jesus has had. He cannot overlook you at this critical period. He sees your dangers. He is acquainted with your temptations. He invites you to follow His example."[22]

Knowing the Jesus was a real, genuine teenager and not a play-acting God, should greatly encourage every young man or woman who is wrestling with the common concerns and natural urges that all teenagers understand well.

Of course, some teenager will still ask, "How did He do it? Sounds impossible!" Now we are face to face with the facts of life or, as some say, where the rubber meets the road. Jesus lived His teenage life as He is willing to help young men and women live theirs! He understood through personal experience the boy-girl stress that any fully alive teenager feels today. That is the whole point of His being our High Priest today: "For we do

---

19. *Ibid.,* 71.

20. ____, *Signs of the Times,* June 23, 1881.

21. ____, *The Youth's Instructor,* August 23, 1894.

22. ____. *Manuscript Releases,* vol. 4, 235.

not have a High Priest who cannot sympathize with our weaknesses, but was in all points tempted as we are, yet without sin. Let us therefore come boldly to the throne of grace, that we may obtain mercy and grace to help in time of need" (Hebrews 4:14–16).

As He drew near the throne of grace daily and refreshed His moral clarity, so we may draw near the same throne, where "this same Jesus" is ready to pour into every teenager's mind the same thoughts and divine energy that He needed to "quench all the darts of the wicked one" (Ephesians 6:16).

Mothers

Some women are no more than biological parents. Children are necessary baggage. But many other women are "mothers" who see in their children their closest mission field. Whichever, there is nothing easy about rearing children. Surprises and disappointments lie around every corner. What to do—is often the helpless cry.

How did mothers 2,000 years ago relate to Jesus? What did they learn from this young Galilean teacher? They soon discovered that Jesus understood their daily load, and they left Him "encouraged to take up their burden with new cheerfulness." They were encouraged when they discovered that He had a mother who "struggled with poverty and privation."[23]

Every mother today can relive the remarkable experience of the Canaanite mother who had more faith in Jesus than did most of His own countrymen. She had a devil-possessed daughter, and Jesus was her only hope. Was He too busy to listen? Hardly. In spite of the urging of His disciples to hurry on, Jesus gave her words that she would never forget: "O woman, great is your faith! Be it done for you as you desire. And her daughter was healed instantly" (Matthew 15:28, KJV).

Or, consider the mother in Nain whose only son had died. Jesus saw the funeral party, paused to take it all in, and told the mother, "Do not weep" (Luke 7:11–17). And He restored the son to his mother. Obviously, people were dying every day in Palestine, and Jesus did not intervene very often. But His special care for mothers was never limited.

Mothers today have the same anxieties, the same weariness, that mothers in Palestine brought to Jesus. "This same Jesus" holds out His hand today to burdened mothers. Mothers today can lift up their children to be blessed by "this same Jesus," who is very close through His Holy Spirit— and the same healing words and touch can be understood and felt today.

---

23. *Ibid.*, 512.

Untold millions of mothers have known what I mean!

Fathers

Think of the high governmental official in Capernaum whose son was very sick. He begged Jesus to come with him to his son's bedside. A few words of hope from Jesus were all he needed, and because of that faith, Jesus had more converts—the father and all his household. This man's faith opened up our Lord's ministry in Capernaum (John 4:46–54).

Think of Jairus, the ruler of the synagogue. His little daughter was dying, and he wanted Jesus to hurry. Before they arrived, the news came that she had died. Our Lord's response: "Do not fear, only believe [Gr. "have faith, trust in Me and the goodness of God]." Soon, amidst the scoffs of the bystanders and the grief of the parents, Jesus took the 12-year-old by the hand and said, "Arise."

Not every son or daughter in Palestine was raised from his or her deathbed. But this "same Jesus" recognized something special in this father—He knew his hurt. Perhaps He remembered—like a hot knife in His own heart—the death of His father, Joseph. And today this "same Jesus" knows the pain in every decent father's heart who stands by his child's bed, powerless in his ability to help. Or fathers who stand at the door, watching teenagers walk down self-destructing paths. The pain in the heart of God has been beyond words since the Garden of Eden, as His sons and daughters have rejected His love and counsel. "This same Jesus" knows all about what fathers with broken hearts feel!

For many of those silent years Jesus watched His father's industry, perseverance, and integrity with customers, and perhaps also his declining strength, as he continued to make a living for his fairly large family. No doubt He relieved His father's stress with song and cheerfulness—just as He will do for every hard-pressed father today who strives to care for his family's needs. "This same Jesus" today hears every father's plea for physical and emotional strength—and the same deep well of encouragement is always there from which to draw.

For all who feel unhonored and unknown

Many parents, many orphans, many teenagers, many single adults often feel that no one cares if they live or die. They produce what is expected and often more. Their only ray of hope is that God is near and that they can still trust Him regardless of earthly circumstances

Further, they may know that Jesus had spent years going through the same misty paths they are now on. I like Ellen's insight:

"For a long time, Jesus dwelt at Nazareth, unhonored and unknown, that he might teach men how to live near God while discharging the humble duties of life. It was a mystery to angels that Christ, the Majesty of Heaven, should condescend, not only to take upon himself humanity, but to assume its heaviest burdens and most humiliating offices. This he did in order to become like one of us, that he might be acquainted with the toil, the sorrows, and fatigue of the children of men, that he might be better able to sympathize with their distresses and understand their trials."[24]

This kind of Jesus, we all need many times in our lives, just to keep our balance and to renew our energy.

---

24. *Signs of the Times*, February 4, 1877.

FIVE

What Difference Does All This Make to Struggling Sinners?

W e know much about how Jesus related to individuals and their particular problems 2,000 years ago. We know how He faced up to sinners who had messed up their lives. And He knew how to deal with human suffering—and with those who were suffocating in their doubts.

But what we need to know is that "this same Jesus" can deal with helpless sinners today. And He can come close to those who are beaten down with suffering and with their doubts. How do we know all this? Because "this same Jesus" is our High Priest in the heavenly sanctuary, whose chief job description is to do what He did while on earth—to give "mercy and . . . grace to help in time of need" (Hebrews 4:14–16)

Someone on the other side of the track

Think of how Jesus dealt with the Samaritan woman at Jacob's well (John 4). No doubt despised by other women in her village, no doubt an easy mark for lusty men, she had come to the well at noon—the time when other women would stay at home. With the eye of a prophet, Jesus saw at a glance the kind of straitjacket she was wrapped in, with no hope of ever being different.

But with His "tact born of divine love," He asked a favor to get her attention. He gently led the conversation, awakening her curiosity; her "bantering manner began to change." She was not used to serious talk, especially from a man. Soon, she was aware of a man who knew her inner soul, her inner dreams that had been well-nigh snuffed out. The more they talked, the more she felt that mysterious touch of the Holy Spirit. She knew that Jesus knew her, inside and out, and she, in turn, shared her confidences. She trusted Him, not only for His analysis of her misdeeds but for His loving understanding—and for the glimmer of a better future. Her true response was revealed in her public testimony—a testimony that must have aroused ridicule at first, then acceptance that something wonderful had happened to her. She evangelized her home town![1]

The lesson for confused men and women today? "This same Jesus" can read your mind too! If there is the slightest whisper that you want radical change in your life—that is the Holy Spirit talking to you. And He wants you to know that "this same Jesus" can give you also a new, guilt-free life of peace and hope. That's His job! That is what He is good at!

Beaten-down Mary

Think of Mary, who seemed never to say No to the many men in her life. Seven times she thought she had found the "right guy." We all know the story of the super-righteous, hypocritical Pharisees with stones in their hands and a terrified woman at their feet. Only Jesus saw the big picture. Only Jesus knew how to really settle the problem that no one could ignore. The forever lesson He gave everyone that day changed the life of Mary to the point she would be the first to announce His resurrection! What was His message? "[Dear One,] neither do I condemn thee: go and sin no more" (John 8:11, KJV).

How many Marys (and yes, their Johns), beaten down with bad choices and who can barely lift their eyes above the pavement, are there in the twenty-first century? How many others are sailing under false pretenses, rearing their families, keeping their smiles, but all the while underneath is the dread that they may be "found out"? They live in quiet horror—their play-acting can't last forever, and everything that they think secure could vanish overnight.

These Marys and Johns today need to talk to "this same Jesus." His eagerness to help you is no different today than it was for terrified Mary centuries ago. He has ways of disentangling you from great embarrassments.[2]

---

1. John 4:39–42

2. "Whatever your anxieties and trials, spread out your case before the Lord. Your spirit will be braced for endurance. The way will be opened for you to disentangle yourself from embarrassment and difficulty."—*The Desire of Ages*, 329.

He has the same inner power available that made struggling Mary into one of His most reliable witnesses.

You say you've tried all this before? So had Mary—seven times! But Jesus never gave up on Mary, and He will not give up on you. He never turns away a weeping, contrite man or woman. "This same Jesus" will be to you what He was to Mary of Magdala.

SIX

What Difference Does All This Make to Those Struggling With Various Temptations?

Who doesn't struggle with various temptations? That question is a no-brainer! What can "this same Jesus" do for struggling church leaders, as well as others, men and women, who are bedeviled with pornography? Or with over-indulgence in eating good food or bad? Or crossing the line with a "fatal attraction"? Or habits with alcoholic beverages or smoking? Or just plain negative, habitual weaknesses such as laziness or gossip, power-hunger, deceitfulness, or being a control freak? The list could go on!

I have discovered that every one of us feels condemned, even by this short list. Is there anything on that list that is more important or worse than another? *What can we do about it?*

Our Lord's faithful disciple John wrote that "For all that is in the world— the lust of the flesh, the lust of the eyes, and the pride of life—is not of the Father but is of the world. And the world is passing away, and the lust of it; but he who does the will of God abides forever" (1 John 2:16, 17).

John later wrote that outside the New Jerusalem would be "dogs and sorcerers and sexually immoral and murderers and idolaters, and whoever loves and practices a lie" (Revelation 22:15).

Paul made sure that his Galatian converts were not confused about the good news of the Gospel. Becoming Christians involved more than a change of day on which to worship and whom they called Lord. No matter

49

what translation one chooses, Paul's message is clear: "I say then: Walk in the Spirit, and you shall not fulfill the lust of the flesh. . . . Now the works of the flesh are evident, which are: adultery, fornication, uncleanness, lewdness, idolatry, sorcery, hatred, contentions, jealousies, outbursts of wrath, selfish ambitions, dissensions, heresies, envy, murders, drunkenness, revelries, and the like; of which I tell you beforehand, just as I also told you in time past, that those who practice such things will not inherit the kingdom of God" (Galatians 5:16–21).

The point of all these texts is to remind us that such is the life of those who are not choosing to be led by the Holy Spirit. No matter how much is covered up so that no one on earth knows of one's moral failures, the time usually comes, even in this life, when it all hits the light of day. But if not in this life, surely on the other side!

The good news is that "this same Jesus" has opened the door to moral energy and stands ready to slam the door leading to these immoral practices for anyone who chooses His help. One thing clear throughout the Scriptures is that rebels, whom John and Paul are describing unambiguously in these verses, are showing the universe that they could not be entrusted with eternal life.

Let's now look at how "this same Jesus" can come to the aid of every one of us afflicted by any of these sinful practices, no matter how satisfying some of them are.

None of us can overlook the nose-to-nose confrontation that Satan had with Jesus, soon after His baptism, in what we call the "wilderness temptations." These are not special temptations that Satan cooked up against his archenemy. We are not observing some kind of intergalactic war, much beyond our personal experience as fumbling human beings. Jesus is fighting temptations that have afflicted every man or woman since Eden.

First, we must get the rules of engagement clear in our minds. Jesus was not facing Satan in as favorable a position as Adam and Eve did. Jesus had taken "man's nature *after* the race had wandered four thousands from Eden, and from their original state of purity and uprightness. Sin had been making its terrible marks upon the race for ages; and physical, mental and moral degeneracy prevailed throughout the human family . . . Christ bore the sins and infirmities of the race *as they existed* when He came to the earth to help man. In behalf of the race, with the weaknesses of fallen man upon Him, He was to stand the temptations of Satan upon *all points* wherewith man would be assailed."[1]

---

1. White, *Selected Messages*, bk. 1, 267, 268 (emphasis supplied).

What have we learned here—conclusions that are based on many biblical texts and other Ellen White commentary:

1. Jesus did not come to earth as a reverse astronaut. He did not come to earth as astronauts go to the moon, fully encased in their space-suits and protected from any contamination they might find on the moon. No, Jesus was born to Mary, with all the genetic liabilities with which all children are born. Ellen White, in her inimitable way, put it this way:

   > *"Like every child of Adam* He accepted the results of the working of the great *law of heredity.* What these results were is shown in the history of His earthly ancestors. He came with such a heredity to share our sorrows and temptations, and to give us the example of a sinless life.

   > "Satan in heaven had hated Christ for His position in the courts of God. He hated Him the more when he himself was dethroned. He hated Him who pledged Himself to redeem a race of sinners. Yet into the world where Satan claimed dominion God permitted His Son to come, a helpless babe, subject to the weakness of humanity. He permitted Him to meet life's peril *in common* with *every human soul,* to fight the battle as *every child of humanity* must fight it, at the risk of failure and eternal loss."[2]

2. About the only advantage Jesus had in dealing with Satan was that He chose His own mother. He grew up as all boys and girls do, learning as fast as His brain matured. And He faced the same kind of enticements to "get even" with his taunting siblings when they wanted Him to join them in their "childish" mischief. Or the same allure of "normal" teenagers with their typical adventures in finding out "what life is all about." In other words, *He was not "exempt" from satanic temptations, either from within or without. He did not share the life of a human who only "vicariously" felt the tugs of temptation.*

3. Satan, giddy with anticipation, remembered all his tricks in leading every human being since Eve to concede to his wiles. When He discovered that Jesus had not come in a space bubble, that He was as vulnerable as any other child, his fiendish glee planned his first major assault—in the wilderness where Jesus had been led by the Holy Spirit to find quietness to think through His earthly mission. Remember, Jesus met life's circumstances as every young man would, and He would need the Holy Spirit, as any serious young person would.

---

2. ____, *The Desire of Ages,* 49.

4. Satan's core attack plan was the same that had overcome all other human beings: His familiar plan was to appeal "through the indulgence of lustful appetite and corrupt passion."[3] That plan is still the shortcut Satan uses today to cause modern men and women to loosen their guard.

Now, let's review how Satan used his usual battle plan on 30-year-old Jesus. In what we call the "first temptation" (Matthew 4:3, 4; Luke 4:2–4), Satan, in the guise of an angel straight from heaven, used his most successful strategy, which has been "to conceal his real purposes, and his true character, by representing himself as man's friend and a benefactor of the race. He flatters men with the pleasing fable that there is no rebellious foe, no deadly enemy that they need to guard against, and that the existence of a personal devil is all a fiction."[4]

Roleplay with Jesus on those fateful days, as He became increasingly tired and hungry. This "angel from heaven" has come to aid you in reaching your objectives. Try to feel the "depth of anguish that fallen man had never realized."[5] Think through as Jesus did, the downward slide of all men and women who had "indulged appetite and . . . unholy passion . . . which had brought upon man inexpressible suffering . . .[that] had been increasing, and strengthening with every successive generation."[6]

How did Jesus "resist the power of Satan's temptations"? "He must show in man's behalf, self-denial and perseverance, and firmness of principle that is paramount to the gnawing pangs of hunger. He must show a power of control over appetite stronger than hunger and even death."[7]

How closely did Jesus come to every beaten-down man or woman? "The humanity of Christ reached to the very depths of human wretchedness, and identified itself with the weaknesses and necessities of fallen man."[8]

As if in answer to His prayers, Satan came enshrouded with light, his words gilded with heavenly harmony. Eloquent Satan "tried to make Christ believe that God did not require Him to pass through self-denial and the sufferings He anticipated; that he had been sent from heaven to bear to Him the message that God only designed to prove His [Christ's]

---

3. ____, *Selected Messages*, bk. 1, 269.

4. Ibid., 270.

5. Ibid., 271.

6. Ibid.

7. Ibid., 272.

8. Ibid., 272, 273.

willingness to endure.. . . . Like Abraham He was tested to show His perfect obedience."[9]

In fact, Satan used a master ploy: He told Jesus that long years ago an
exalted angel had been exiled to Planet Earth and that Jesus, in His present emaciated, distressed appearance, was that fallen angel—and that Satan, a comforting Angel of Light and Power, could help Him reach His objectives.

All of this transpired over a number of days. I wish we had been given
more information as to how this lengthened conversation went from day
to day. Ellen White's insights add to the abbreviated description that Matthew and Luke have given us.

What is evident is that the first satanic temptation included far more
than the prospect of a good meal. Of course, it is natural for Christ to want
to eat after many days of fasting.

But more than a duel over eating is going here. Every God-given appetite (desire and passion for physical comfort, fellowship with the opposite
sex, and for self-worth), however, had been distorted into a frenzy of unin-
hibited craving the world over and in all times.

Self-gratification is the will of God turned upside down. That leads us to
the eternal lesson we can learn in Christ's response to this subtle, powerful
temptation. To give in to desire, craving, and lust of anything that conflicts
with the will of God for our well-being, is to set up a chain of habits that
will take us captive. But Jesus has shown us that nothing "is more important than that bearing upon the control of the appetites and passion."[10]

You ask, how did Jesus, with no advantages over other men and wom-
en, pull it off and turn Satan into a boiling fury? Matthew tells us: "Jesus
was led up by the spirit into the wilderness to be tempted by the devil"
(Matthew 4:1). Jesus could never have endured all that stress, mentally
and physically for forty days, if He tried to beat Satan with his own human wit.

Stung by Christ's response to his persuasive appeals, Satan regrouped
and worked next with a different temptation (Matthew 4:5–7). Still the
Angel of Light, he takes Jesus to the top of the temple in Jerusalem. First,
he commends Jesus for His "fidelity" and now His "steadfastness." But this
time he focuses on another human weakness—that of the "believer" who
wants God's help without full commitment to God's expressed will. We

---

9. Ibid.

10. ____, *The Desire of Ages*, 122.

call it presumption, wherein we place ourselves in situations that ask for God's protection, as if we are asking for help that He has not promised.

Many call their presumption, faith. It is not faith that expects the favor of God in circumstances that God cannot bless. For Jesus to test the favor of God would show the universe that He did not see through Satan's slick temptation—that He did not know the rest of the text that Satan quoted—words that clearly spelled out the faithful obedience that sincere children of God would place first in any temptation.

The point here is that whenever Satan sets up a situation where we place ourselves unnecessarily in the way of temptation, he knows he has won.

Though licked again, Satan did not give up. The third temptation showed a different strategy. No longer in the guise of a messenger from heaven, He reappears as a mighty angel and as the leader and god of this world. He knows that Jesus is very weary, weak, and emaciated.

Taking Jesus to a very high mountain (no one knows where), in some kind of astrophysical display, Satan laid out the beauty and possibilities of this earth without the traces of sin. Some contrast to the rugged, forlorn wilderness that He had been in for close to forty days! "All this I will give you and its glory if, if Thou wilt worship me." In other words, it would be all Christ's—all the honor and all the glory.

But Satan still did not understand. Jesus came to set up a kingdom, but it was founded on integrity, fairness, and righteousness.

Jesus had given Satan every opportunity to shoot his most powerful guns. No one anywhere in the universe could say that Jesus was afraid of Satan's cleverness, so that He couldn't face evil face-to-face, as He expects all created intelligences to likewise do. No one will ever say that Satan was not given a fair chance to prevail in His face-to-face encounter with Jesus, his archrival.

What does this all mean to us today?

1. Paul understood all this well: "Above all, taking the shield of faith with which you will be able to quench all the fiery darts of the wicked one" (Ephesians 6:16). What we see in Satan's signature temptations are the three core "darts" (temptations) with which Satan zings all of us.

2. Ellen White has spelled it out well: "Many look on this conflict between Christ and Satan as having no special bearing on their own life; and for them it has little interest. But within the domain of every human heart this controversy is repeated. . . . The enticements,

which Christ resisted, were those that we find it so difficult to withstand. . With the terrible weight of the sins of the world upon Him, Christ withstood the test upon appetite, upon the love of the world, and upon that love of display which leads to presumption. These were the temptations that overcame Adam and Eve, and that so readily overcame us"[11]

3. Some say that we are in a different position than Christ, because as God, He could not be overcome by temptation. But as we have said earlier, if Jesus had not become a human being like the rest of us, "then He would not be able to succor us. But our Saviour took humanity, with all its liabilities. He took the nature of man, with the possibility of yielding to temptation. We have nothing to bear which He has not endured."[12]

4. In fact, Jesus had a greater burden resting on Him then we ever can have or adequately understand. Jesus, with the same human liabilities that all human beings have had, was fighting "the battle as every child of humanity must fight it, *at the risk of failure and eternal loss.*"[13] "He took the nature of man, with the *possibility of yielding to temptation.*"[14] When we stand on the Sea of Glass and are overwhelmed with the glory of heaven, "we shall remember that He left all this for us, that He not only became an exile from the heavenly courts, but for us took the *risk of failure and eternal loss.*"[15]

Can anyone reading this page fully understand this? Of course not! But again, this is not a mere history lesson! He did all this, and it is recorded for us, so that we would get serious about our own confrontations with the evil one. Sin, for Jesus, was as eternally consequential as it is for us today!

5. So often today we hear that we have nationality weaknesses, neighborhood challenges, family-line weaknesses, etc. Anything to excuse our seared habit patterns. We let psychology precede theology in our thinking: We let philosophical excuses determine the kind of Saviour we want to believe in. In other words, don't make Jesus too much like ourselves, for then we won't have any excuses!

---

11. Ibid, 116, 117.

12. Ibid.

13. Ibid., 49 (emphasis supplied).

14. Ibid., 117 (emphasis supplied).

15. Ibid., 131 (emphasis supplied).

But Jesus blanked out all those human excuses: "Only by the inexpressible anguish which Christ endured can we estimate the evil of unrestrained indulgence. His example declares that our only hope of eternal life is through bringing the appetites and passions into subjections to the will of God."[16]

6. One of the great lessons I learn from Christ's wilderness temptations is the great importance that appetites of all kinds (such as for scrumptious food, alcoholic beverages, smoking, resisting exercise, etc.) and God-given passions (sexual activities, comfort, and self-worth) should be under the control of a person's will, that is given over to the Holy Spirit for moral strength.

7. When Jesus said that the "prince of this world" found nothing in Him (that is, after doing his mighty best, Satan could not get Jesus to sin), it simply means that Jesus did not respond to Satan's coy enticements. Jesus did not consent to sin, and that is why He is called the "sinless Savior"—not because He was born with special advantages not available to the rest of us, but because He never chose to sin. But then we are told: "So it may be with us. Christ's humanity was united with divinity; He was fitted for the conflict by the indwelling of the Holy Spirit. And He came to make us partakers of the divine nature. So long as we are united to Him by faith, sin has no more dominion, over us. God reaches for the hand of faith in us to direct it to lay fast hold upon the divinity of Christ, that we may attain to perfection of character."[17]

Now let us get back to our chapter's topic. How does knowing that "this same Jesus" of the wilderness temptations makes any real difference in our lives today? This much I do know:

1. If Jesus did not have a regular, consistent prayer life, He never would have been our world's Redeemer! Paul instructs us as to why Jesus prayed! He prayed for the Holy Spirit to help Him when in the clutches of satanic temptations:

> "Who in the days of His flesh, when He had offered up prayers and supplications with vehement cries and tears to Him who was able to save Him from death, and was heard because of His godly fear, though He was a Son yet He learned obedience by the things He suffered" (Hebrews 5:7, 8).

2. If anyone has ever doubted our Lord's full acceptance of the

---

16. Ibid., 122.

17. Ibid., 123.

humanity with which we are born, then Paul's words should eliminate any further reason to doubt. Here, Paul tells us why "this same Jesus," described in verses 7 and 8, "earned the right"[18] to be our High Priest and is now able to "sympathize with our weaknesses, but was in all points tempted as we are, yet without sin" (Hebrew 4:15).

3. The Greek word for "prayers" is a specific word for "special, definite requests." Throughout His earthly journey, from His youngest years until Calvary, Jesus had the same needs for which to pray as we do today. Read carefully:

> "The same grace given to Jesus, the same comfort, the more than mortal steadfastness, will be given to every believing child of God, who is brought into perplexity and suffering, and threatened with imprisonment and death, by Satan's agents. Never has a soul that trusts in Christ been left to perish. The rack, the stake, the many inventions of cruelty, may kill the body, but they cannot touch the life that is hid with Christ in God."[19]

3. Note that Jesus needed a daily prayer life for Himself and for others:

> "While the city was hushed in silence, and the disciples had returned to their homes to obtain refreshment in sleep, Jesus slept not. His divine pleadings were ascending to His Father from the Mount of Olives that His disciples might be kept from the evil influences which they would daily encounter in the world, and *that His own soul might be strengthened and braced for the duties and trials of the coming day.* All night, while His followers were sleeping, was their divine Teacher praying. . . . *He prayed for His disciples and for Himself, thus identifying Himself with our needs, our weaknesses, and our failings, which are so common with humanity.* . . . Christ is our example. Are the ministers of Christ tempted and fiercely buffeted by Satan? So also was He who knew no sin. He turned to His Father in these hours of distress. He came to earth that He might provide a way *whereby we could find grace and strength to help in every time of need, by following His example in frequent, earnest prayer.*"[20]

4. To put it as clearly as I can, Jesus "needed grace" daily. While on

---

18. ____, *The Desire of Ages*, 745.

19. ____, *Signs of the Times*, June 3, 1897; *Seventh-day Adventist Bible Commentary*, vol.5, 1123.

20. ____, *Amazing Grace*, 167.

earth, He needed prayer, gathering "to Himself power to resist evil and to minister to the needs of man. . . . He knows the necessities of those who, compassed with infirmity and living in a world of sin and temptation, still desire to serve Him."[21]

So how will "this same Jesus" hover close to you as He did with His disciples, who too were often confused, weak, and sometimes defeated?

1. Bring your prayers to Jesus, even as often as you breathe.

2. Bring your prayers to Jesus, not to test Him but to trust Him.

3. Bring your prayers to Jesus, knowing that He asked for help from the Holy Spirit to meet the same temptations that you now face.

4. Bring your prayers to Jesus, knowing that He has already promised you "mercy and to find grace to help in time of need"—exactly what He prayed for 24/7.

5. Bring your prayers to Jesus, knowing that the same help He received in His own trials and temptations—the same words of encouragement the Holy Spirit gave Him—He now stands ever ready to give you.

I am not talking religious fantasy. The whole plan of salvation, the integrity of the universe, rests on these simple truths about how men and women resist the devil. Jesus did not resist the same devil because He was somehow programmed before He came to earth never to sin. He resisted in the same humanity you and I have. If what I am now writing is pure poetry without any reference to reality, then the promises of Jesus and the biblical writers are a mere hoax to induce self-hypnotism!

Perhaps now we can face up to the underlying truth that shapes our battles with temptations. The Lord can step in with mental and moral clarity only when we open the door to His help. That closed door is personal disobedience to the light of truth we all have. Not everyone has the same amount of light, obviously. But all have enough light to make moral decisions and to open that door, enabling "the same Jesus" to say to us today: "Neither do I condemn you; go and sin no more" (John 8:11).

Not to open that door is to remain in frustration and in the mere twilight of unrepented sins.

We all must ask ourselves this question: Is there anything in my life that I am intentionally holding onto that is bracketed by 1 John 2:16: "For all

---

21. Ellen G. White, *The Acts of the Apostles*, 56.

that is in the world—the lust of the flesh, the lust of the eyes, and the pride of life—is not of the Father but is of the world?"

Of course, everyone will say Yes! *That is why we need to be converted daily!* And the Lord's promise is: "If we confess our sins, He is faithful and just to forgive us our sins and to cleanse us from all unrighteousness" (1 John 1:9).

In other words, the Lord can help us when we open the door to His mercies. Let these words burn within you as you read:

> "He who repents of his sin and accepts the gift of the life of the Son of God, cannot be overcome. Laying hold by faith of the divine nature, he becomes a child of God. He prays, he believes. When tempted and tried, he claims the power that Christ died to give, and overcomes through His grace. This every sinner needs to understand. He must repent of his sin, he must believe in the power of Christ, and accept that power to save and to keep him from sin. How thankful ought we to be for the gift of Christ's example!"[22]

That's right! Jesus came and died to give us each both mercy and grace to be an overcomer. *"This, every sinner needs to understand!"* In other words—Believe it, Accept it, and Live it!

No mystery here! In this simple formula, "the same Jesus" is saying that when you see Him again, you will see Him in peace, because you have, in your days of probation, recognized the unvarnished truth on which the future of the universe depends: "Then men and women will see that the prerequisite of their salvation is obedience to the perfect law of God. None will find excuse for sin."[23]

Make this your daily prayer, breathed often, in private or in public:

"Thank You, Lord Jesus—You went through a lot to guarantee us life forever. You have faced up to the evil one, as no other human being has ever done. You have shown us that we can face up to the same evil one only by truly permitting the Holy Spirit to do for us what He did for You. Please, Lord, give me a clear eye as to what sin really is in my life today. Help me to hate it as You hated sin. Help me to make a habit of hating sin—any sin, large or small. I know I cannot do this hating without the Holy Spirit helping me to hate sin as He helped You. Please, Lord, make me to be a living witness who helps You to settle the Great Controversy, here and now and forever. Amen."

All this is His living promise. "This same Jesus," who forgave and

---

22. ____, *Selected Messages*, bk. 1, 224.

23. Ibid., 225.

empowered men and women 2,000 years ago, is ready to open a new chapter in our lives today, and tomorrow, and forever.

For the past six years I have been watching this whole chapter unfold in the lives of two young people who, about seven years ago, were known around the city of Lincoln, California, as druggies and alcoholic bums. He graduated from high school as valedictorian and was appointed for West Point. She was also a bright student, whose father was mayor of their city.

But in the summer after graduation, life took a terrible turn—a life that lasted for twenty-five years. She was in jail three times as a drug dealer—anything to get more drugs. He had different jobs in the construction trade, highly regarded as a keen worker. For relaxation, he became a rock music entertainer.

With Susan in jail for the last time—and Rich was on the outside, they both finally hit rock bottom. In their desperation, and knocking at death's door, they cried out to God for help. Their prayers were answered. Their obsession to use drugs and alcohol was lifted. Now, instead of searching for drugs, they began searching for truth.

One day by chance, while working at Taco Bell, she recognized a new customer to be Doug Batchelor, speaker on the Amazing Facts television program. A remarkable relationship developed. She and her partner soon realized that their life depended on finding the true God and making a complete change in their lives. Their only alternative, they realized, was to listen carefully to Pastor Batchelor's encouragement. As the months went by, they attended the Sacramento Central Seventh-day Adventist Church, week after week, with their long, scraggly hair, dingy overalls (without adequate funds), and flip-flops. The church nurtured them.

Soon they were baptized. Never again have they looked back. Today, they have significant jobs worthy of their intellectual ability. She devotes Fridays to schools through the county that ask for her lectures on "overcoming addiction."

Through all this "growing up," they met several Adventist couples with whom they became fast friends. This began a remarkable outreach-witnessing program that began in their own home. Who comes? Many of the co-workers who work with this "new man in Christ Jesus." Already, at least four families have followed them in baptism—happy overcomers of the dreaded chains of addiction.

Our little church of Lincoln, California, has grown from a handful in 2002 to approximately 120 worshipers, largely built on the Sabbath lesson studies and this former rock musician's sermons. Remarkable sermons— as clear and as deep as those of the best minister anywhere.

What is going on here? These two are simply witnesses to the promises that we have been reviewing in this chapter. To hear them talk about Jesus and the Holy Spirit invigorates us all. Humbly, they decry their twenty-five years of utter self-gratification. They rarely even talk about their experiences in any detail. They know there is nothing positive in so doing. They wince when they hear music in worship services that reminds them of the beat of satanic music that enthralled them for years.

At the present time, they conduct a public "recovery from addiction" program on Thursday nights, with a steady increase of friends who invite *their* friends, who want the victories that they see in these two leaders.

All who watch this last-day drama unfold must recognize that if "this same Jesus" can loosen the chains of satanic habits called "addiction," He can also rescue those who are addicted with gossiping, with meanness to those with whom they disagree, with "control over others" problems, and with the addiction of always wanting to "be right"!

"This same Jesus" is very good at what He does, when He is asked to help. Perhaps someone, as he or she reads these lines, feels the urge to reach out for His help. The Holy Spirit makes you feel that way, and the Holy Spirit will be to you what He was to Jesus of Nazareth—full of grace to overcome the evil one, whatever the "dart" may be. Let Him give you the joy of overcoming, even in the sins that most other people know nothing about. And for those sins that others surely know about, give them another witness to "the same Jesus" that my two friends in Lincoln, California, are giving to all who know them.

SEVEN

What Difference Does All This Make to Those Who Suffer?

One great lesson Jesus made clear was that God is not responsible for suffering. That surely was a new thought, not only to His disciples and fellow Jews, but to all the world. Remember how confused the friends of Job were, blaming his troubles on an offended God?

In John 9, on a pleasant Sabbath day, Jesus and His disciples were passing a blind man, which prompted a question from one of the disciples: "Rabbi, who sinned, this man or his parents, that he was born blind" (verse 1)? No question about it, someone had sinned—and God was punishing this man!

Jesus was emphatic: neither this man nor his parents had sinned! Which leaves the question in the air for a while. But He did say that He would make something good out of this distressing situation: "[I will see to it] that the works of God might be made manifest in him."

Of course, all suffering and death happen because of someone's transgression of God's moral or physical laws. But Satan perverted this truth. He did a remarkable job of placing the blame back on God, even though he, Satan, is the author of sin and its consequences. Probably most of the billions on earth today believe that God, for some reason, is the instigator of all suffering and death. They haven't read the Book of Job.

Luke recalls another incident when Jesus had to clarify the truth about calamities and sufferings. In referring to those killed by the collapse of the Siloam tower, Jesus was again emphatic: The dead were no more sinners than anyone else in Jerusalem (Luke 13:1–5). Whenever Jesus had the opportunity, He repudiated the popular notion that suffering is a direct intervention of God to somehow get even with sinners. It is always a temptation for too many to treat accidents or misfortune as confused insurance companies do, declaring so many sad events to be "an act of God"! This is a thundering lie!

A thundering lie

I have been a pastor of several churches and also a school administrator for many years. I wish I had never had to listen to so many fathers and mothers and friends in general who were smothered in confusion regarding the suffering and death of loved ones.

However, "this same Jesus," who cleared up this age-old lie in His day, wants everyone, anywhere today to get the facts straight once and for all time to come: God is the Author of life and restoration; Satan is the author of sin, suffering, and death. God is the Restorer and Lifegiver! Satan is the destroyer![1]

Where, then, is God when we suffer? He's exactly where He was when Jesus was suffering in Gethsemane and on the Cross. Jesus said it well: "An enemy has done this" (Matthew 13:28). Our Lord used the recent episode of the traveling Samaritan in hostile territory to make an unforgettable point: The Samaritan stopped when a priest and a Levite (religious leaders, of all people) "passed by on the other side." Why? Because "he had compassion." Like a laser beam, Jesus shot home His lesson: "Go and do likewise" (Luke 10:37).

Feeling with one's gut

Many times gospel writers noted our Lord's compassion for the suffering. Our English word *compassion* is a weak translation of the Greek word describing "feeling with one's gut." It is translated in other English passages as "affection," "sympathy" (see Philippians 2:1), or "his heart goes out to you" (2 Corinthians 7:15). This Greek word is an amazing description of how deeply Jesus feels for others, then and now, when they are suffering. More than mere sympathy (a weak translation), Jesus feels with His gut. We all know the feeling. Think back to when you have been under great stress, and recall the response of your intestines. When we get that focused on the sufferings of others, then we can say that we are truly "compassionate."

---

2. *The Ministry of Healing*, 113.

Untold millions of Christ's loyalists have either discovered the truth about "this same Jesus" in their suffering (beating Satan at his own game) or have held their head high as evil men and women destroyed their bodies but not their spirit.

One tragic day in Blacksburg, Virginia, on the campus of Virginia Tech, thirty-three people were killed, including the murderer. April 16, 2007 will be forever etched in our memories, not only at Virginia Tech but around the world, as the day this black evil unfolded.

A few days later, at the Crystal Cathedral in Garden City, California, Virginia's Governor, Tim Kaine, reflected on the tragedy: "It is really important, I think, that God sent Jesus to Earth so He could draw closer to us, so He could understand human suffering, and what a comfort it is to know that our Creator has also experienced the loss of His only child, and that can make us very close together in times of grief and sadness."

Finding God in a Gulag

Charles Colson wrote a fascinating book called *Loving God,* in which he relates one of the most fantastic stories I've ever heard.[2]

He tells of a Jewish Russian physician. He had been sentenced to a gulag, one of many in the dreaded Russian concentration camps. We don't know what his crime was, except that it was political. Now, to be a Jewish physician in the Soviet Union suggests that he must have been in sympathy with Communism. After all, most of the Jews in the Soviet Union fell in with Communism for a very simple reason: For more than 200 years they had been persecuted by professed Christians, with the blessing of the czars. A glimpse of their misery may be gained from the unforgettable film *Fiddler on the Roof.*

One of the top officials in the Christian church in Russia once said, "We need to kill one-third of the Jews, imprison another third, and see that the other third leave the country." Against that backdrop, you can see why Communism would appear to Jews as salvation from Christian oppression.

So it must have appeared to Boris Nicholayevich Kornfield, M.D. But at some time he apparently questioned Stalin and had been sentenced to the gulag. Reflect for a moment—physicians in a prison camp care for everyone, including the commander and guards, as well as the other prisoners. Thus physicians are treated with deference in comparison with other prisoners. After all, who would want to be operated on by a surgeon who hates

---

2. Grand Rapids, MI: Zondervan Publishing House, 1983, 27–34.

you and might let you bleed to death as his knife slipped? So Boris must have enjoyed some favors other prisoners never saw.

One day he talked to a patient who said he was a Christian, that he believed the Bible, that he believed in God's Messiah, and that Messiah was a suffering Jew. The patient talked of his sufferings as being unworthy to compare with the sufferings of God's Messiah. But Boris had never felt he deserved any of the suffering that he himself was going through. He had an intense hatred for Christians and for all that had been done in their Christ's name against his people.

Yet he saw in the man a quiet confidence and conviction he had seen in no one else. Very quietly, very secretly, Boris accepted Jesus Christ to be his Messiah.

Implications of accepting Christ

Dr. Kornfield began to think about all the implications of this new commitment. He examined his own life. For instance, it was routine that before any prisoner could be put in solitary confinement, a physician had to sign a form and say he was physically in good shape—certificates that nearly always were lies. Most men died in solitary confinement—and he had signed hundreds of such forms.

But now Boris decided that as a Christian, he could no longer lie in preparing those forms. In this resolve never to lie, he knew he would be signing his own death warrant.

One day in the hospital ward Boris saw men dying of diseases from which they could have survived, had they only had food! After seeing one such prisoner die he walked out into the hall, only to see an orderly—a turncoat prisoner—eating the bread that had been intended for the sick patients. Boris reported the orderly to the commandant.

The commandant was amused. "All right," he said, "we'll put the orderly in solitary confinement for three days." The compassionate physician knew that when that orderly got out of solitary, he would be as good as dead.

One afternoon a few days later, Boris Kornfield walked into his hospital ward and saw a patient who had just been operated on for cancer. He was used to seeing sorrow in faces, but there was a sorrow and a depth of sensitivity in this face that he had seen in no other prisoner. So Boris sat beside this total stranger and poured out what had happened in his own life—how he was a Jew, how he had become disillusioned with Communism, how he had embraced God's Messiah, how he had seen that he could no longer sign the solitary confinement warrants, and how he knew he had only a very short time to live.

But he said, "I feel freer than any man in the Soviet Union, and I feel a joy I never knew existed." Boris was finding a deeper meaning to life, because he identified with the Suffering Messiah. And as God would have it, "this same Jesus" was imparting wisdom to him—that deeper meaning that Jesus Himself had learned while on earth.

What about that patient to whom Kornfield poured out his soul? He was in and out of consciousness in that recovery room as the anesthesia wore off. But he was fascinated by the physician's comments. He held on to every word. Somehow, he stayed awake.

Later that night, the recovering patient listened for Dr. Kornfield to return as usual. Again the next morning, he waited for this remarkable physician. But Dr. Boris Kornfield never returned. When he had left his patient that previous afternoon, as he stepped into the hall, he was struck in the head eight times. He was dead the next day.

Alexsandr Solzhenitsyn

But the patient Dr. Kornfield had talked to was Alexsandr Solzhenitsyn, who learned the story of the ages about a Suffering Messiah from the converted Jew. From this Jewish physician, Solzhenitsyn found a source of hope and power that molded him into becoming the moral beacon to hundreds of thousands of fellow Russians—to hold on a little longer.

After Solzhenitsyn's release from the Gulag, he was eventually expelled from Russia because he spoke so loudly, so eloquently, against the inhumanity and meaninglessness of Communism. In his visits to America, he raised his voice against western decadence and loss of purpose and meaning to life.

But there is more to Solzhenitsyn's story. After he recovered from his surgery he rejoined the prisoners in their work programs. Prisoners were not allowed to speak! Further, they were forbidden to read! Solzhenitsyn said that the strain and repression became overwhelming. He thought, *I will never get out of here.* So he planned how he would end his life. He knew that if he tried to escape, he would be shot; and he wrote, "that would be the end of that."

The next day he was taken, as usual, with the other prisoners out to work. When a break came, he sat down under a tree. He even placed his hand against the tree, ready to push off and run. He would be shot and put out of his misery. Just then a shadow came across the grass. A fellow prisoner sat down beside him. Although forbidden to speak, he could at least look into the eyes of other prisoners. The two men locked eyes. Solzhenitsyn saw something he had rarely seen in any face—a message of love and concern.

Cross in the sand

Then the other prisoner took a step forward, and with a stick in his hand drew a cross in the sand. New hope surged. Thoughts of God flooded Solzhenitsyn's mind: *God has not forsaken me. He loves me. He is in charge.* For weary Alexsandr there was still hope—and he would live on.

Would you believe, three days later, without any warning, he was released from that prison? At his release, he learned that many people had been praying for him. He now knew for sure that he had reason to hope and to live on.

And so Solzhenitsyn did, giving us some of the greatest literature of the twentieth century. Who gave that unknown prisoner the wisdom to draw the cross in the sand? And who implanted the meaning of the cross in Solzhenitsyn's mind? The same Holy Spirit who prompted "this same Jesus" day and night. As our High Priest, Jesus knew exactly what Alexsandr Solzhenitsyn needed in the worst of times in twentieth-century Siberia. Fellow sufferers recognize fellow sufferers! And Jesus, the Great Sufferer, is very good about what He does!

EIGHT

What Difference Does All This Make to Those Who Doubt?

Everyone doubts at some time in his or her life. Christians, at times, doubt their assurance of God's promises. In crises, even Christians, at times, wonder where God is.

Jesus was a master at dealing with all kinds of doubts. Interesting that "doubt" comes from the Latin meaning "two." Other languages describe doubt as "having a foot in two boats," or "having two thoughts," etc. The Greek words translated "doubt" in our English Bibles describe those who are torn between two opinions, or unable to make up one's mind, or debating with himself or herself, or hanging back.

But we must remember that doubt is not the absence of faith—doubt is the space in between faith and unbelief. Too many feel guilty when they have doubts, but that is unfair. *Unbelief* is simply the refusal to believe— doubt wavers. There is no such thing as "total doubt." Contradiction in terms! But we must be alert to do something about doubts before they become settled unbelief.[1]

And that is where genuine faith comes in. Faith does not believe what is not so! Faith has confidence in God that leads to obedience to whatever that pleases God. One of the problems besetting doubting Christians

---

1. I am indebted to Os Guinness for this insight. See *God in the Dark* (Wheaton, IL: Crossway Books, 1996).

is that some may not have a clear picture of what God is really like. Some believe that God's will is done in whatever happens on earth—and that can be crushing to most of us. Some believe that God is too busy to get involved in every detail of every Christian's life. Some believe in God-talk and know their Bibles well, but they do not personally "know" God as a personal Friend.

In Mark 9 a father asked Jesus to heal his demoniac son. Jesus replied that all things were possible for those who believe (the Greek word is better translated "have faith"). The father immediately shouted his plea: "Lord, I believe [have faith]; help thou mine unbelief [lack of faith]." We all have cried that prayer sometime in our lives.

Wavering faith not unbelief

Here is a good example of Jesus responding, not to unbelief, but to one who was wavering under the awful stress of a boy out of control. Jesus would not have responded if He thought the father did not believe that Jesus could help in some way. Jesus always responds today to those, like that distressed father, whose doubts are like "a wave of the sea driven and tossed by the wind" (James 1:6).

Remember when Jesus, after His resurrection, appeared to the disciples while they were hiding perhaps in their favorite upper room? Some of them had actually seen their resurrected Lord, and now they were listening to the two who had walked to Emmaus with Jesus. And while all this was being discussed, Jesus appeared, and they were "terrified and frightened, and supposed they had seen a spirit" (Luke 24:37).

Then, after looking at His hands and feet, "they yet disbelieved not for joy, and wondered" (verse 41). What is going on here? Just shows that "unbelief" or "disbelief" sometimes describes doubts of genuine believers who should know better. At times, emotions often overpower reason and evidence in the best of us.

Something else happened to Peter, as he sank in the lake after his attempt to walk to Jesus. Jesus responded: "O thou of little faith, wherefore didst thou doubt" (Matthew 14:31, KJV). Jesus was not spanking him for wanting to walk on water. The Greek word Jesus used, here translated as "doubt," describes one who is hesitating or faltering. In other words, "Peter, why did you waver, when you already were doing well?"

Doubt happens in many ways

I hope you are getting the point. Doubt happens in many ways. The core problem is that doubters look at their doubts instead of to God, whom they should be trusting and obeying. The facts are, as we all know through personal experience, that no real trust happens without obedience to known duty! That is why Jesus said to Peter, "Have faith in God" (Mark 11:22, KJV). A literal translation would be: "Keep on trusting God's faithfulness." The best way to resist doubt is to build up trust in God. Too many of us spend time and energy fighting our doubts.

Remember how Jesus handled "doubting" Thomas (John 20:26–29)? Thomas had abundant proof that Jesus was now alive. Granted, he had not been at the tomb on Sunday morning, and for some reason he had not been with the disciples when Jesus appeared on Sunday night in the upper room. My guess is that he was nursing his disappointment of missing out on a literal earthly kingdom that he thought Jesus was about to set up. Perhaps it was his wounded pride—that Jesus had revealed Himself to all the other disciples but not to him.[2]

A week later, Jesus appeared again with the disciples, and Thomas was there. During that long week, Thomas had been salving his feelings by saying that he would not believe unless he, himself, could touch Jesus' wounded hands and feel His punctured side. Amazing pout! First of all, he wouldn't take the witness of his closest friends at face value. More amazing! But he had not yet settled into unbelief. He was still wavering—he wanted to be with the disciples once more.

Jesus knew all this, and He made the point of speaking directly to Thomas' ambivalence: "Thomas, put your finger in my scars, in my hand and in my side, but please do not be faithless, renew your faith" (verse 27). We do not know if Thomas ever reached out to fulfill his bravado, but we do know that he probably fell at the feet of Jesus saying, "My Lord and my God!"

I am glad that John had reported this remarkable moment for all disciples to share, then and now. Jesus accepted Thomas' acknowledgement, but He nailed down a great lesson for all men and women ever since: "Thomas, because you have seen Me, you have believed. Blessed are those who have not seen and yet have believed" (John 20:29).

After all, those Jews and Gentiles who had never seen or heard Jesus listened to the good news of the apostles—and ever since, everyone who made Jesus their Lord did so through the witness of others. Where would any of us be today if we insisted that our doubts would be cleared up if we could see and hear Jesus for ourselves? Such is the blessed mystery of the Christian church—we believe today on the basis of someone else's faith!

---

2 _____, *The Desire of Ages*, 807.

That is how the gospel has always spread, even in our own day—"from faith to faith" (Romans 1:17).

Anatomy of some doubts

This incident was reported by John to show the anatomy of doubt, even by a loyal disciple. Thomas' feelings were hurt, he was disappointed that the pathway that Jesus took did not go the way he had dreamed, and he demonstrated his reluctance to believe because he didn't have the experience that others had. Recipe for spiritual disaster! What if Thomas had chosen not to meet with the disciples on that second Sunday evening?

In these New Testament episodes we see how Jesus related to various kinds of "doubting." We all have experienced one or more of these types of doubt. What we do know for sure is that "this same Jesus," who satisfied scared parents, over-confident Peter, and troubled Thomas, will be the "same Jesus" for you in your dark moments in your Christian journey.

Pilgrim's Progress

Remember how John Bunyan pictured doubt in *Pilgrim's Progress,* with Christian traveling with Hopeful on their journey to the "King of the Celestial Country": Christian and Hopeful erected a sign to keep other pilgrims from falling into the hands of Giant Despair: "Over this stile is the way to Doubting Castle, which is kept by Giant Despair, who despiseth the King of the Celestial Country, and seeks to destroy his holy pilgrims. Many therefore that followed after, read what was written, and escaped the danger."[3]

Doubt is debilitating. Doubt is not a sign of rational thinking. Doubt is forgetting the kind of God running the universe. Doubt forgets that "this same Jesus" is our High Priest, who will supply all the reasons for genuine faith. That's our Lord's job, in His role as our "all-powerful Mediator.

"Everyone who will break from the slavery and service of Satan, and will stand under the blood-stained banner of Prince Immanuel will be kept by Christ's intercessions. Christ, as our Mediator, at the right hand of the Father, ever keeps us in view, for it is as necessary that He should keep us by His intercessions as that He should redeem us with His blood. If He lets go His hold of us for one moment, Satan stands ready to destroy. Those purchased by His blood, He now keeps by His intercession."[4]

Believe it! Trust Him! Jesus is very good at what He does!

---

3. *The Harvard Classics,* vol. 15, 123.

4. White Comments, *SDA Bible Commentary,* vol. 6, 1078.

NINE

What Difference Does All This Make to Those Facing Death?

W e are emphasizing that "this same Jesus," who walked this earth 2,000 years ago, is our very-much-alive High Priest in the heavenly sanctuary, as the Book of Hebrews makes so clear. In fact, that is the major theme of Hebrews!

Then we ask, so what? What difference does that mean to us today? Much in every way! Jesus lived the same kind of human experience that we face daily. Note how Hebrews expressed it: "Inasmuch then as the children have partaken of flesh and blood, He himself likewise shared in the same. . . . Therefore, in all things He had to be made like his brethren ["in every respect," RSV], that He might be a merciful and faithful High Priest. . . . For that He Himself has suffered, being tempted, He is able to aid those who are tempted" (2:14, 17, 18).

And to make sure that we got the point, this awesome fact that "this same Jesus" is in heaven as our High Priest is repeated in chapter four: "For we do not have a High Priest who is cannot sympathize with our weaknesses, but was in all points ["every respect," RSV] tempted as we are, yet without sin. Let us therefore come boldly to the throne of grace, that we may obtain mercy and find grace to help in time of need" (4:15, 16).

Never alone

No matter how many times I read these texts, I get goose pimples! I keep pausing to say, "Thank You," throughout the day and night—especially during the night hours! Because "this same Jesus" is alive, day and night, by the throne of God as our "all-powerful Mediator," we never need to worry or wonder about going through life alone. We are never alone! And that means, whatever the situation may be, Jesus through the Holy Spirit and mighty angels is ready to forgive and to supply the power of grace to help in our hour of need! That is an out-of-this world arrangement that only God could think up!

Further, it means that Jesus experienced the same joys and sorrows we do, the same pitiful human situations we get into, the same subtle temptations that catch us by surprise. And He wants us to ask, "How did He do it?" How did He get "grace to help in time of need?"

He did it by sharing with His Heavenly Father and the Holy Spirit the challenges He faced daily—the same challenges we all face. And He received mental and moral clarity through His close abiding with them both—just as He promises to give us the same kind of mental and moral help in our daily challenges, if we continue to abide as a branch abides in the vine.

Facing death of others

Yes, Jesus had His very special friends. He found in the home of Lazarus and his two sisters a refuge where He could "speak with simplicity and perfect freedom, knowing that His words would be understood and treasured."[1] Perhaps a quiet retreat away from even His disciples!

Here he could help Martha be more like Mary, and Mary to be more like Martha! But then came that awful day when Jesus received the news that Lazarus was desperately ill. Strange, His disciples thought, that Jesus was in no hurry to rush to Bethany! But after two days He led them to Bethany, saying, "Don't worry, men, Lazarus has fallen asleep." When the disciples understood that to mean Lazarus had recovered, Jesus spoke even more plainly, "Lazarus is dead" (John 11:14).

Now, this is something new for everyone concerned! Before they had even arrived in Bethany, Martha was down the road looking for Jesus. Lazarus had already been "in the tomb four days." She wanted our Lord's comforting hand and words. Mary's first words were those of deepest friendship and trust: "Lord, if you had been here, my brother would not have died" (verse 32). No anger, no resentment—just sharing her confidence in her friend, Jesus.

---

1. ____, *The Desire of Ages*, 524.

How did Jesus respond to all this grief and heartache? "He was deeply moved in spirit and troubled. . . . Jesus wept" (verses 33, 35).

What's going on here? Jesus could have healed Lazarus as He had others for several years. Yet He actually permitted Lazarus to die! Why? He wanted to do something for his Bethany friends and for His disciples that they would never have understood fully, if He merely lectured to them about the sleeping dead. This was real compassion!

And the three Bethany friends and the disciples would look back on Lazarus' resurrection with thankfulness and wonder, telling the story of 1) the unforgettable compassion and empathy of Jesus—"this same Jesus" who has the same compassion, feeling, and empathy for those today who grieve—and 2) the thrilling reason to trust Jesus to be the great Lifegiver when He returns.

So today, we know that "this same Jesus" still "weeps with those that weep, and rejoices with those that rejoice."[2]

Facing one's own death

But what about facing one's own death? Has Jesus given us any special help here? Does "this same Jesus" have anything truly helpful and practical when we face our own death?

Gethsemane and Calvary are wells without bottoms when we try to understand why Jesus died. But they also tell us how to face death!

Death, for most people, is a black door that few want to go through. It happens to somebody else. Most people don't want to be around when it happens! That's why so many postpone making their wills or living trusts.

The facts of life are that death is not an old person's disease. It can happen anytime! How should committed Christians who believe their Lord's promises face death?

Gethsemane and Calvary were not slam-dunks for Jesus. He was not programmed as if He were a robot. I know He had more on His mind than anyone else who has ever lived and died. After all, the way He faced death had much to do with how everyone today faces death. Whatever His choice in Gethsemane, it had eternal implications for you and me today.

Rejected by everyone

Remember, Jesus was still in battle with Satan. Satan knew how to press his case against Jesus—His own special people had rejected him, His own

---

2. Ibid., 533.

disciples were still confused about His mission, and He had no earthly reason to believe that He should permit Himself to be crucified.

Three times He wrestled with all the issues at stake! He longed for human sympathy, even from one person who could pray with Him with a hand on His shoulder. He was let down by His closest friends, even John. Alone, "He prayed for His own tempted, agonizing soul."[3]

Even the angels in heaven were wrapped in "silent grief." The future of the universe pivoted on our dying Lord, who could leave Gethsemane and fight Satan some other way, if possible. But the third prayer, called forth from the depth of pending despair, convinced a mighty angel who took Lucifer's place in heaven, that Jesus had settled into His decision to beat Satan down, whatever the cost. That angel did not remove the "cup from Christ's hand, but strengthened Him to drink it, with the assurance of the Father's love."[4] His evening of agony had been paying the price of satisfying justice, outguessing Satan as to how justice and mercy could be reconciled if and when forgiving sinners were confused as to how God could be just and still forgive. Gethsemane and Calvary settled the confusion that God was unjust and unfair.

Throughout that awful night, Jesus was subjected to every insult, every abuse, that the malignity of evil men could devise. He had even held out His hand to Judas, hoping that in this late hour he would see his awful folly, but Judas realized it was "too late."

Further, Jesus could have manifested His divine character, but that would not have been what other men and women could do in the same circumstance. His disciples crept around in the shadows, not wanting to arouse suspicion! No one stood up for Him! Amazing!

Where was Satan through it all? He was hoping that someone would finally provoke Jesus enough so that He would perform a miracle and cause the authorities to release Him. And that would be worth all the horrid attempts he had made to cause Jesus to stumble during the last thirty-three years.

How did He do it?

Through it all, hour after hour, suffocating on the cross, blood poisoning racing up his arms and legs, the one last barrier against utter despair was "the evidence of His Father's acceptance. He was acquainted with the

---

3. Ibid., 690.

4. Ibid., 693.

character of His Father. . . . By faith He rested in Him whom it had ever been His joy to obey. . . . By faith, Christ was victor."[5]

Jesus taught us how to die under the worst of circumstances! Hundreds of thousands of martyrs through the centuries rallied their courage by remembering how their Lord died for the sake of truth. Whatever the circumstances, however that day comes to us all (and we all will die, if not translated), "this same Jesus" will remind us of the same evidence His mind processed as He approached Gethsemane and endured the Cross.

When the body begins to fail, when the mind wanders, when medications no longer seem to be sufficient for our needs, when few seem to grasp what is really happening—you still have the companionship of "this same Jesus," who knows exactly what your mind needs to hear. Trust me when I say you can trust Him. That's why He is our High Priest today, who is able "to sympathize with our weaknesses" and who asks us to draw "boldly to the throne of grace, that we may obtain mercy and find grace to help in time of need" (Hebrews 4:15, 16).

---

5. Ibid., 756.

TEN

What Difference Does All This Make to Those Facing the Evil One?

If Jesus came down without being born of Mary, Satan would have retreated, knowing that he should bide his time until Jesus returned to heaven. No contest—they both would forfeit the game. And no one would have really won! Humanity would have continued to deteriorate in every way. The world would end in any number of ways, as evil genius would keep inventing new ways for men and women to destroy one another. The last one to die would turn off the lights.

God foresaw all that! That is why He intervened. He wanted men and women to see some hope in the dismal future—and some reason that the future could be changed, at least for those who chose to accept counsel from their Creator.

That's why Jesus became a human being! Not only to show us how much God loved men and women, not only to satisfy justice in His plan to redeem the willing, but also to show, in flesh and blood, that a human being could stand up to Satan, regardless of how mean and furious and crafty he could be.

When John tells us that the willing redeemed will "conquer" the Evil One, even as Jesus did (Revelation 3:21), the first question is: How did He do it?

Reality check

But first, our reality check! Our Lord Jesus did not come to this earth to show the universe that God could keep God's laws. *He came on Satan's turf to do battle with him just as every man or woman must face Satan:*

> "But when Adam was assailed by the tempter, none of the effects of sin were upon him. . . It was not thus with Jesus when He entered the wilderness to cope with Satan. For four thousand years the race had been decreasing in physical strength, in mental power, and in moral worth; and Christ took upon Him the infirmities of degenerate humanity. Only thus could He rescue man from the lowest depths of his degradation. Many claim that it was impossible for Christ to be overcome by temptation. . . . If we have in any sense a more trying conflict than had Christ, then He would not be able to succor [help] us. But our Saviour took humanity, with all its liabilities. He took the nature of man, with the possibility of yielding to temptation. We have nothing to bear which He has not endured."[1]

So, how did He do it? Remember in the wilderness experience (Matthew 4), that at no time did Satan give any visible clue that he was anyone other than a very sympathetic, loyal, unfallen angel. He came with all the assurances that he was there to help and support Jesus as He began His public ministry. In this remarkable setting, Jesus went toe-to-toe with Satan, His former friend who turned evil.

▸ Jesus relied on His understanding of the Old Testament Scriptures and on the spoken words of His heavenly Father, who had recently said, "This is My beloved Son, in whom I am well pleased" (Matthew 3:17).

▸ Jesus did not put Himself into a position that would suggest that His heavenly Father should come to His rescue; that is, to test God to prove God's reliability.

▸ Jesus recognized the difference between faith and presumption; faith, for Jesus, rested on the "promises and provisions of the Scriptures."[2]

▸ Satan knew, by studying our Lord's DNA that was passed on to Him through His mother's genetic stream, exactly what His hereditary weaknesses were ("that He took humanity with all its liabilities"); nevertheless, Jesus rejected the enormously subtle temptations of

---

1. *The Desire of Ages,* 117.

2. Ibid., 126.

submitting to appetite, the love of the world, and the love of pretentious display.[3]

▸ How does this help us? No mystery here—do what Jesus did!

▸ Regardless of circumstances, regardless of how difficult life's choices may be, regardless of what may seem to be "good" reasons to relax our commitments to our Lord—"trust in the Lord with all your heart and lean not on your own understanding" (Proverbs 3:5). Trust His Word. His Word is very powerful; it once spoke into existence this world at creation. His Word resurrected Lazarus. Do what Jesus did—He relied on powerful words of Scripture. You too can trust its promises!

▸ When the night is dark and clouds come in, you cannot see where North is— keep trusting that the needle can. Don't put yourself into compromising positions, hoping that the Lord can extricate you. That is presumption, not faith.

▸ Don't make excuses for yourself! Don't cover up your personal responsibility by saying, "That's just my nationality," Or, "That runs in my family." We all have genetic weaknesses, as Jesus had, but the Holy Spirit's job is to help us overcome all these hereditary weaknesses—all of them![4] And He is very good at what He can do!

Now, again, how does this help us today? "This same Jesus" who needed the daily empowering of the Holy Spirit, "this same Jesus" who relied on the Scriptures for daily strength, will give us today the same insights and power He needed to overcome the Evil One and all inherited weaknesses.

I know it is truly amazing that a Man with the same inherited weaknesses as we all have could have resisted Satan. Not even by a thought did He yield: "So it may be with us. . . . He was fitted for the conflict by the indwelling of the Holy Spirit. . . . So we may resist temptation, and force Satan to depart from us. Jesus gained the victory through submission and faith in God."[5]

We are not merely discussing interesting theological subjects—as, for example, how the tithe should be used. What Jesus is doing now, and the

---

3. Ibid., 116, 117.

4. *Christ's Object Lessons*, 330.

5. *The Desire of Ages*, 123, 130.

difference that should make for each of us, determines the kind of joy or despair we face each day or night. All Jesus wants is an opportunity in our lives to make the difference that we deeply want but don't know how to pull off.

ELEVEN

What Difference Does All This Make to the Lonely?

I know it sounds strange to think that the Creator of heaven and earth, the Lord of millions of adoring and respectful angels, would ever be lonely! Yes, those of us who do battle with the stress of life and live among self-oriented people, even family members—yes, we can understand why so many men and women and boys and girls live lonely lives. For some, loneliness seems to be their lot, especially when they commit their lives to obeying and honoring their Lord Jesus—and then watch family and friends fade away.

Does the Jesus of the Bible have something to say to lonely people today? I'll say He does! He talks from experience—a lifetime of loneliness. Nobody today should ever be so alone that he or she cannot hear the Voice of One who cares. I like the way Ellen White said it:

> "Whatever our situation, if we are doers of His word, we have a Guide to direct our way; whatever our perplexity, we have a sure Counselor; whatever our sorrow, bereavement, or loneliness, we have a sympathizing Friend. If in our ignorance we make missteps, the Saviour does not forsake us. We need never feel that we are alone. Angels are our companions. The Comforter that Christ promised to send in His name abides with us. . . . There is not a sorrow, not a grievance, not a human weakness, for which He has not provided a remedy."[1]

---

1. Ellen G. White, *The Ministry of Healing,* 248, 249.

83

How do we know that Jesus understands what loneliness really is? Because He lived a life surrounded by loneliness, from the time of early childhood until His ascension. "No one upon earth had understood Him, and during His ministry He must still walk alone. Throughout His life His mother and His brothers did not comprehend His mission. Even His disciples did not understand Him."[2]

"No fun anymore"

I know people who have come very close to this kind of loneliness. After they found a new life and vigor in their new walk with Jesus, even their family, their parents and children, wrote them off as "no fun anymore."

Think how you would have felt if "through childhood, youth, and manhood,"[3] no one fully understood your devotion to principle and to the God you read about in Holy Scriptures, even as Jesus focused on the God He saw revealed in Scripture.

God the Father knew the kind of utter loneliness Jesus was going through. "Bearing the weakness of humanity, and burdened with its sorrow and sin, Jesus walked along in the midst of men."[4] That is why He sent Moses and Elijah to meet with Him on the mount we call Transfiguration. He saw and felt the awful weight resting on Jesus. Of course, Jesus had the cool breeze of the Holy Spirit night and day. Of course, the Father could have sent angels to encourage Jesus. But the Father knew exactly what Jesus needed—He sent two great men of faith who also had "endured suffering and sorrow, and who could sympathize with the Saviour in the trial of His earthly life."[5]

Why Moses and Elijah?

Why Moses and Elijah? Because these two men had known loneliness, and they had seen the unspeakable reward for staying the course, no matter how bleak and desolate one's path may be. They were the best voices in the entire universe of created intelligences to speak courage to the lonely Jesus!

Think of our Lord's Gethsemane loneliness—a loneliness no man or woman will ever have to endure. No martyr dying in fire at the stake, or with a rope around his neck, or stretched out on a rack, or facing boil-

---

2. ____, *The Desire of Ages*, 111.

3. ____, 92.

4. ____, 422.

5. Ibid.

ing oil or a firing squad—ever felt this kind of loneliness, because they could die with a song on their lips. Each one knew that Jesus had gone through a deeper loneliness and that He was now passing on to them the same kind of inner strength on which He had rested. But of all heroes of faith, Jesus alone could whisper, "I have trodden the wine press alone" (Isaiah 63:3).

Why am I emphasizing the lifelong loneliness of Jesus? Because "this same Jesus" knows exactly what comfort we need today. Untold numbers of people have learned the truth of the following promise: "Whatever our situation, if we are doers of His word, we have a Guide to direct our way; whatever our perplexity, we have a sure Counselor; whatever our sorrow, bereavement, or loneliness, we have a sympathizing Friend."[6]

Two Babes in a Manger

In 1994, the story is told of two Americans who had answered an invitation from the Russian Department of Education to teach in Russia. They were invited to teach at many places, including a large orphanage. About one hundred abandoned and abused boys and girls were in the care of a government-run program.

Near the holiday season, it seemed appropriate for the visiting Americans to tell the traditional story of Christmas—about Mary and Joseph arriving in Bethlehem.

Finding no room in the inn, the couple went to a stable, where Baby Jesus was born and placed in a manger. Throughout the story, the children and orphanage staff sat in amazement as they listened. Soon, they sat on the edges of their seats, trying to grasp every word.

The teachers tell the story: "Completing the story, we gave the children three small pieces of cardboard to make a crude manger. Each child was given a small paper square, cut from yellow napkins I had brought with me. No colored paper was available in the city.

"Following instructions, the children tore the paper and carefully laid strips in the manger for straw. Small squares of flannel, cut out from a worn-out nightgown an American woman was throwing away as she left Russia, were used for the baby's blanket. A doll-like baby was cut from tan felt we had brought from the United States.

"The orphans were busy assembling their manger as I walked among them to see if they needed any help. All went well until I got to one ta-

6. _____, *The Ministry of Healing*, 248, 249.

ble, where little Misha sat. He looked to be about six years old and had finished his project.

"As I looked at the little boy's manger, I was startled to see not one, but two babies in the manger. Quickly, I called for the translator to ask the lad why there were two babies in the manger.

"Crossing his arms in front of him and looking at this completed manger scene, the child began to repeat the story very seriously. For such a young boy, who had only heard the Christmas story once, he related the happenings accurately—until he came to the part where Mary put the Baby Jesus in the manger.

"Then Misha started to ad-lib. He made up his own ending to the story, as he said, 'And when Maria laid the baby in the manger, Jesus looked at me and asked me if I had a place to stay. I told him I have no mama and I have no papa, so I don't have any place to stay. Then Jesus told me I could stay with Him. But I told Him I couldn't because I didn't have a gift to give Him like everybody else did.

" 'But I wanted to stay with Jesus so much, so I thought about what I had that maybe I could use for a gift. I thought maybe if I kept Him warm, that would be a good gift.

" 'So I asked Jesus, 'If I keep You warm, will that be a good enough gift?' And Jesus told me, 'If you keep Me warm, that will be the best gift anybody ever gave me.'

" 'So I got into the manger, and then Jesus looked at me and He told me I could stay with Him—for always.'

"As little Misha finished his story, his eyes brimmed full of tears that splashed down his little cheeks. Putting his hand over his face, his head dropped to the table, and his shoulders shook as he sobbed and sobbed.

"The little orphan had found Someone who would never abandon or abuse Him. Someone who would stay with him—for always."

The teacher summed up her thoughts: "I've learned that it's not what you have in your life, but Who you have in your life, that counts."

Little Misha, in some deep experience, discovered the truth that Baby Jesus was "this same Jesus" who spoke to Him through the Bethlehem story. That's part of our Lord's job description as our Most High Priest in the heavenly sanctuary today.

Of course, Baby Jesus grew up, as all boys and girls do, but He knew a loneliness that no other person has ever experienced. Some come close, perhaps, but never has anyone been as lonely as Jesus was for thirty-three years!

That is why I can write with energy and confidence that whatever the thoughts were that daily encouraged and empowered lonely Jesus from childhood to Calvary, "this same Jesus" is waiting to give the same messages through the Holy Spirit to us. That's what His being our merciful High Priest is all about!

Remember the job description of "this same Jesus" when He became our High Priest: "We have not a High Priest who is unable to sympathize with our weaknesses, but one who in every respect has been tempted as we are, yet without sinning. Let us then with confidence draw near to the throne of grace, that we may receive mercy and find grace to help in time of need" (Hebrews 4:15, 16, RSV).

TWELVE

What Difference Does All This Make to Those Facing Career Choices?

Not many men or women have a clear picture of what they should do in life. And if they do embark on a career that fits their native abilities, they are still subject to the wiles of others who can imperil the well-being of even the most diligent worker. Evil lurks around every career corner. If anyone thinks they can outsmart envy or jealousy, they have surprises waiting for them. How does "this same Jesus" become the daily solution to career difficulties that hundreds of thousands of honest men and women face constantly?

Remember that day when two trusted disciples asked Jesus, " 'Teacher, we want You to do for us whatever we ask.' And He said to them, 'What do you want Me to do for you?' They said to Him, 'Grant us that we may sit, one on Your right hand and the other on Your left, in Your glory.' But Jesus said to them, 'You do not know what you ask. Are you able to drink the cup that I drink'" (Mark 10:35)?

What is going on here? James and John had missed a lot of what Jesus had been teaching, in word and by example. They said, "We are able!" Jesus then told them that such career aspirations are to those "for whom it has been prepared." What about the other ten disciples? They were "indignant at James and John" (verses 40, 41).

This kind of interchange goes on every day, in every business establishment, in every governmental office, and among church officials on any level of responsibility.

Principle that scuttles the power-hungry

What principle did Christ teach that scuttles every ambitious, power-hungry man or woman? "But it shall not be so among you; but whoever would be great among you must be your servant, and whoever would be first among you must be slave of all" (verses 43, 44).

"This same Jesus" wants every modern disciple to listen to this principle today.

He knows that not everything is crystal clear as one plans his or her life work. Or when occasions arise when moves are necessary in one's organization, but you are passed over, even though qualified. Or when a supervisor seems to ignore one's accomplishments but is quick at finding fault. What then?

"This same Jesus" has much to quiet our consternation: "When we are born from above, the same mind will be in us that was in Jesus, the mind that led Him to humble Himself that we might be saved. Then we shall not be seeking the highest place."[1]

How then does one get "promoted"? We must stand back and watch for God's leadings:

> "Our plans are not always God's plans. He may see that it is best for us and for His cause to refuse our very best intentions, as He did in the case of David. But of one thing we may be assured, He will bless and use in the advancement of His cause those who sincerely devote themselves and all they have to His glory. If He sees it best not to grant their desires He will counterbalance the refusal by giving them tokens of His love and entrusting to them another service. In His loving care and interest for us, often He who understands us better than we understand ourselves refuses to permit us selfishly to seek the gratification of our own ambition. He does not permit us to pass by the homely but sacred duties that lie next us. Often these duties afford the very training essential to prepare us for a higher work. Often our plans fail that God's plans for us may succeed."[2]

Sooner or Later

We all must, sooner or later, listen to this counsel: "The Lord has no place in His work for those who have a greater desire to win the crown than to bear the cross. He wants men [and women] who are more intent upon doing their duty than upon receiving their reward,—men [and women] who are more solicitous for principle than for promotion. . . . If they

---

1. Ellen G. White, *The Desire of Ages*, 330, 331.

2. ____, *The Ministry of Healing*, 473.

are qualified for a higher position, the Lord will lay the burden, not along on them, but on those who have tested them, who know their worth, and who can understandingly urge them forward."[3]

I could wish that many more would learn this sooner than later. It would save us many nights of anguish, many days of stress. Jesus knew this early:

"The Son can do nothing of Himself" (John 5:19). Even Jesus on earth knew that "we [including Himself] have not wisdom to plan our own lives. It is not for us to shape our future. . . . Christ, in His life on earth made no plans for Himself. He accepted God's plans for Him, and day-by-day the Father unfolded His plans. So should we depend upon God, that our lives might be simple outworking of His will"[4]

"This same Jesus" stands ready today to pass on the lessons of life He learned as the humble Christ 2,000 years ago. He watched men and women plan with hard work for their futures but "make an utter failure." We all have seen that success is never final!

Many times young and old have seriously asked me: "What should I do in life? It seems that I could go down different roads, but I am not sure." Most frequently I would lead them to page 267 in *Education,* the clearest counsel I have ever read regarding career choices. Think about the following points:

▸ "The specific place appointed to us in life is determined by our capabilities."

▸ "Each should aim just as high as the union of human with divine power makes it possible for him to reach."

▸ "Many do not become what they might, because they do not put forth the power that is in them."

▸ "Seeking greater honor or a more pleasing task, they attempt something for which they are not fitted."

▸ "There are others, again, who might have filled a responsible calling, but who, for want of energy, application, or perseverance, content themselves with an easier place."

▸ "We need to follow more closely God's plan of life. To do our best in the work that lies nearest, to commit our ways to God, and to watch for the indications of His providence,—these are rules that insure safe guidance in the choice of an occupation."

---

3. Ibid., 477.

4. Ibid., 478, 479.

These basic principles cut through many pages (and hours) of untold numbers of books on vocational counseling. So much is helpful, but none that I have seen carve out these basic principles any clearer than what we have just read.

It is more than interesting to note that, generally speaking, a person has no more than three choices in determining his or her life work. Our "capabilities" lie primarily in one of three dimensions—the philosophical, the scientific, or sales orientation. We do best what we like best. And we like best what we do best. Two laser beam tests!

But to be successful in the philosophical world, such as a teacher or preacher, that person should have a healthy mix of the scientific mind, as well as the salesperson appeal—such as philosophical, 50 percent; scientific, 25 percent; and sales, 25 percent. A molecular biologist would be configured differently—such as 50 percent to 80 percent scientific; philosophic, 10 percent to 20 percent; sales, also 10 percent to 20 percent. A public relations specialist should have a mix of 50 percent to 60 percent sales; 20 percent to 30 percent philosophical, and 10 percent to 20 percent scientific.

In other words, no one succeeds in being 100 percent of what he or she likes most. Why? A lawyer needs a scientific mind to craft his logical arguments, a philosophical component to weigh motives and form his jury appeal, and a sales appeal to hold attention and "sell" his case before a judge or jury. A preacher should be at least 50 percent philosophical, with insightful thoughts, but if s/he did not have a good mix of the scientific mind, s/he would have administrative difficulties as well as disorganized sermons. And s/he did not have a good sales appeal, s/he would soon have a diminished congregation.

I think of Christ's preparation for His three years of ministry. He spent nearly thirty years in common, mechanical labor. He understood the basic principle: "do our best in the work that lies nearest, to commit our ways to God, and to watch for the indications of His providence." In preparation for greater work, Jesus built up His mental, social, and moral faculties. He understood that one's first responsibility was to be self-sufficient and not dependent on the hard work of others. He learned early that life does not pass out "free lunches."

But that was not all. "This same Jesus," who stands ready day and night to help us, knows exactly what men and women must learn today, regardless of age:

"Jesus did not shirk care and responsibility, as do many who profess to be His followers. It is because they seek to evade this discipline that so many are weak and inefficient. They may possess precious and amiable traits, but they are nerveless and almost useless when difficulties are to be met or obstacles surmounted. The positiveness and energy, the solidity and strength of character, manifested in Christ are to be developed in us, through the same discipline that He endured. And the grace that He received is for us."[5]

I like that! Jesus knows the price of being responsible. He remembers what He needed every day from the Holy Spirit to meet "difficulties" and "obstacles"—just as we do today. And that same character response—"the positiveness and energy, the solidity and strength of character"—"are to be developed in us." How? "Through the same discipline that He endured. And the grace that He received is for us." That is a promise from the "same Jesus" now in heaven as our High Priest. What do you need today? You get what He has promised! And He is very good at fulfilling His promises!

Sooner or later, if we individually ever find peace on this planet, this promise should become our life breath: "God never leads His children otherwise than they would choose to be led, if they could see the end from the beginning and discern the glory of the purpose which they are fulfilling as co-workers with Him."[6]

---

5. *The Desire of Ages*, 73.

6. Ibid., 224, 225.

THIRTEEN

What Difference Does All This Make to Those Seeking Happiness?

J esus said that He had come to Planet Earth to give weak, troubled men and women "life . . . more abundantly" (John 10:10). Millions upon millions would like to believe that promise today. Perhaps you who read this page have only a glimmer of what that promise means—for most, it is no more than poetic fantasy.

But I am not talking about a fantasy that only a few aspiring cover girls seem to have, or the gold that an Olympian champion may have won, or the rich and famous who seem to have everything. Physical beauty, world acclaim, several mansions, and huge holiday bonuses—obviously these assets do not guarantee happiness. Just read the stories of their lives!

In our Lord's remarkable prayer shortly before He led His disciples across the Brook Kedron to the Garden of Gethsemane, He prayed for you as well as for His disciples. That's right—for you and me: "These things I speak in the world, that they may have My joy fulfilled in themselves. . . . I do not pray for these alone, but also for those who will believe in Me through their word" (John 17:13, 20).

Think about it! Here Jesus had you on His mind when He wished your life to be full of joy!

Is there a difference between joy and happiness? Let's talk about it!

Joy seems to be a scarce commodity. Happiness, however, is more often the prize that most everyone seeks. A good night's sleep? So take a pill! A vacation in Hawaii? So use the credit card!, Forbidden pleasures? So take a chance! Whenever happiness is measured by thrills and bank accounts, one never gets enough!

Many Christians say they are abiding in Christ, but few show that they are living "abundantly."

Joy is not a passing emotion such as happiness may create. Happiness may last for a night or a few weeks—but never makes one "full." Happiness depends on happenings. The joy Jesus gives is not fleeting, not a high emotion riding the crest of a wave—it doesn't depend on "happenings."

Joy is not created by possessions or by positions but by a Person. Joy is not something that a sovereign God deposits in minds that claim they have "been saved" without any call for character transformation. But it can be eclipsed by our own disobedience. We all know how true that is!

Joy has two conditions: *submission* and *service.* Jesus used the grapevine to illustrate submission: "Abide in Me, and I in you. As the branch cannot bear fruit of itself, unless it abides in the vine, neither can you, unless you abide in Me" (John 15:4). If we refuse to "abide," (submit) in Jesus, we will no longer bear fruit (service). But "If you abide in Me, and My words abide in you, you will ask what you desire, and it shall be done for you. By this My Father is glorified, that you bear much fruit; so you will be My disciples" (John 15:7, 8).

Joy is maintained by abiding in Him, by believing in Him, by obeying Him. Jesus knew all this personally. "This same Jesus" learned how to anchor His life in the joy of abiding in His Father's will. This kind of abiding joy motivated the young man from Nazareth to become the greatest Person who has ever lived, the revered Savior of the world.

We can never forget Paul's urging to fix our attention on "this same Jesus": "Looking unto Jesus, the author and finisher of our faith, who for the joy that was set before Him enduring the cross, despising the same, and has sat down at the right hand of the throne of God" Hebrews 12:2).

What prompted Jesus to keep going, never faltering, always abiding in His Father's will? It was the joy of submission and service.

But wait a minute. Joy, in hanging naked at the heat of the day on cruel Calvary? Joy, with His closest friends running away because they could not stand the test? Joy, with no visible signs that His thirty-three years amounted to anything? Joy, dying between two criminals? Would you count that joy?

Moment by moment, through all that evil men and Satan himself threw at Him, Jesus knew that He was cooperating with His Father's will. That was His joy!

"This same Jesus" is talking to you as you read. He is reminding you that you will never have to go through a darker or tougher day than He did. What the Holy Spirit was whispering to Him from Gethsemane to the middle of the day on Friday, He will whisper to you when you go through your darkest and toughest hours. In the quiet sense of cooperating with God, you too will find joy.

His shame would mean glory for the redeemed. His humiliation would show the whole universe of intelligent beings that Satan cannot throw anything at our Lord's followers that will take away their joy of submission and service.

Jesus had something special to say about happiness as well as joy. In the fifth chapter of Matthew we have His list of what brings "true happiness." The Greek word often translated "Blessed" was understood by our Lord's audience as "happy."

▶ "Happy are those who know they are spiritual poor; the Kingdom of heaven belongs to them!"

▶ "Happy are those who mourn, God will comfort them!"

▶ "Happy are those who are humble; they will receive what God has promised!"

▶ "Happy are those whose greatest desire is to do what God requires; God will satisfy them fully!"

▶ "Happy are those who are merciful to others; God will be merciful to them!"

▶ "Happy are the pure in heart; they will see God!"

▶ "Happy are those who work for peace; God will call them his children!"

▶ "Happy are those who are persecuted because they do what God requires; the Kingdom of heaven belongs to them!"

▶ "Happy are you when people insult you and persecute you and tell all kinds of evil lies against you because you are my followers. Be happy and glad, for a great reward is kept for you in heaven."[1]

At first glance, with perhaps two exceptions, this "list" doesn't sound very happy to the modern ear. Some would say, "Happy are the unhappy," would be a good summary.[2] But this is our Lord's basic program—this describes the people who will make up His eternal kingdom. It is our Lord's signature profile of people who can be entrusted with eternal life.

When we look at the "list" again, we see the Lord describing people who at the moment are clearly not happy. Some may be especially miserable! But in their misery Jesus is uplifting the secret of joy through it all. That is exactly what He is doing for you who may be living in "unhappy" happenings or circumstances. Keep on abiding in Him, and He will see to it that you will understand the joy that passes all understanding.

My favorite author understood all this well. Circumstances for her were at times miserable. But note her encouragement to others:

> "God has provided for every one pleasure that may be enjoyed by rich and poor alike—the pleasure found in cultivating pureness of thought and unselfishness of action, the pleasure that comes from speaking sympathizing words and doing kindly deeds. From those who perform such service the light of Christ shines to brighten lives darkened by many shadows."[3]

This counsel can be summed up in a few words, wherein she said that Christians are to "find their happiness in the happiness of those whom they help and bless."[4]

Unfortunately, Christians, as well as their Lord, have been accused of being joyless—wet blankets and spoil-sports. This is Satan's propaganda. If Christians are really joyless, then they don't know their Lord very well! When they don't, they turn the truth upside-down by becoming like the "joyless god" they worship!

Listen to this clear picture:

> "There are many who have an erroneous idea of the life and character of Christ. They think that He was devoid of warmth and sunniness, that He was stern, severe, and joyless. In many cases the whole religious experience is colored by these gloomy views. It is often said that Jesus wept, but that He was never known to smile. Our Saviour was indeed a Man

1. *The Good News Bible* (HarperCollins Publishers) is a reliable translation that strives to give readers today maximum understanding of the content of the original texts.

2. Thomas Cahill, *Desire of the Everlasting Hills* (New York: Doubleday, 1999), 77.

3. White, *Selected Messages*, bk. 1, 87.

4. White, *Acts of the Apostles*, 12.

of Sorrows, and acquainted with grief, for He opened His heart to all the woes of men. But though His life was self-denying and shadowed with pain and care, His spirit was not crushed. His countenance did not wear an expression of grief and repining, but ever one of peaceful serenity. His heart was a wellspring of life, and wherever He went He carried rest and peace, joy and gladness."[5]

That is the portrait of "this same Jesus" who is leaning over the ramparts of the heavenly sanctuary, ready to reproduce Himself in you—a cheerful reflection of genuine joy.

Polycarp, Bishop of Smyrna, understood the joy of listening to "this same Jesus." Born in Smyrna about A.D. 69, he soon became a devoted student under the Apostle John, who lived close by in Ephesus, where John spent his retiring years before being sent to Patmos. The record indicates that Polycarp, in many ways, reflected John's noble Christian spirit, full of gentleness, yet inflexible in speaking out against error.

We remember our Lord's message to the church in Smyrna, as written down by John in Revelation 2:8–11. No doubt Polycarp read this Scripture often to his church members. It must have been precious to Smyrnians who were hauled off to face wild beasts or the fiery stake by the Romans who feared another "god" that rivaled Caesar.

Finally, the Roman authorities came for Polycarp. He was recognized as a leader in the city, known for his community service. But hate and fear overruled respect. Acting responsibly, he hid in farmhouses until the authorities found a young boy who knew where he was. The slave boy was horribly tortured until he revealed Polycarp's hiding place. Though escape was still possible, Polycarp refused to put anyone else in jeopardy and surrendered.

He invited his pursuers to share food with him and spoke cordially with them. And then he was led away.

Surrounded by the jeering, hostile crowd in Smyrna's stadium, the Roman proconsul ordered Polycarp to renounce Jesus Christ and give obedience to Caesar as Lord. The proconsul personally did not want this crisis to go any further, pleading, "Consider thyself, and have pity on thy own great age."

He then urged: "Swear, and I will release thee—reproach Christ!"

Polycarp answered: "Eighty and six years have I served Christ, nor has He ever done me any harm. How, then, could I blaspheme my King

---

5. _____, *Steps to Christ*, 120.

who saved me? You threaten the fire that burns for an hour and then is quenched; but you know not of the fire of the judgment to come, and the fire of eternal punishment. Bring what you will."

Three times the proconsul's herald proclaimed to the stadium crowd that Polycarp had professed himself a Christian. The wild uproar demanded his death by the wild beasts, but it was too late in the day for the beasts to be rounded up. So the unanimous shout was that Polycarp should be burned alive.

The records indicate that many in the crowd rummaged the city looking for wood and anything else that would burn. When they were fastening Polycarp to the stake, they wanted to nail his hands, but he countered: "Leave me as I am; for he who giveth me strength to sustain the fire, will enable me also, without your securing me with nails, to remain without flinching in the pile."

History records that the fire burned furiously but did not harm Polycarp, forcing the proconsul to order death by dagger. So on February 23, 155, Polycarp died repeating no doubt the Lord's promise to the Smyrnians: "Be faithful until death, and I will give you the crown of life" (Revelation 3:10).

Did he understand Christian joy? I don't think he was concerned about happiness while the flames engulfed him, but kept "looking unto Jesus, the author and finisher of our faith, who for the joy that was set before Him endured the cross, despising the shame" (Hebrews 12:2).

That's the open secret for those who really want to know why "this same Jesus" ministers in the Most Holy Place for people like Polycarp and you and me. You and I today have no brighter future than to be found by keeping this joy of Jesus in our hearts.

I remember the day when Norma and I walked the streets of Oxford, England, to find that hallowed ground where the Oxford martyrs—Bishops Hugh Latimer and Nicholas Ridley, and Archbishop Thomas Cranmer—were burned at the stake. Latimer and Ridley on October 15, 1555—and Cranmer on March 21, 1556. No statue marks the exact spot, only a modest plaque set into the road opposite Balliol College, where the street narrows. Nearby, however, an imposing stone monument rises at the intersection of St. Giles', Magdalen, and Beaumont Streets.[6]

The inscription at the base of the Martyr's Memorial reads:

6. Kirsopp Lake, translator, *Apostolic Fathers*, Vol. II, Loeb Classical Library, 1911.; *The Catholic Encyclopedia*, Vol XII, (New York: Robert Appleton Company, 1911).

"To the Glory of God, and in grateful commemoration of His servants, Thomas Cranmer, Nicholas Ridley, Hugh Latimer, Prelates of the Church of England, who near this spot yielded their bodies to be burned, bearing witness to the sacred truths which they had affirmed and maintained against the errors of the Church of Rome, and rejoicing that to them it was given not only to believe in Christ, but also to suffer for His sake; this monument was erected by public subscription in the year of our Lord God. MCCCCXLI."

For us, this was an especially quiet and thoughtful moment amidst the roar of afternoon traffic. We remembered the dying words of brave, 70-year-old Ridley, as he prayed aloud: "O Heavenly Father, I give unto Thee most hearty thanks for that Thou has called me to be a professor to Thee, even unto death. I beseech Thee, Lord God, take mercy upon this realm of England, and deliver the same from all her enemies."

Close by, brave 62-year-old Latimer shouted to Ridley: "Be of good comfort, Master Ridley, and play the man! We shall this day light such a candle in England as I trust shall never be put out!"

Six months later, at 67, Archbishop Cranmer, who had tremendous influence on the affairs of kings and queens, was burned in the same ditch as Ridley and Latimer. However, the interesting feature of Cranmer's last days was his repudiation of his submission to the Pope and to Roman Catholic doctrine. As with most all Anglicans, Cranmer was dedicated to Paul's principle in Romans 13:1–5 that we are "subject to the governing authorities. For there is no authority except from God."[7]

Cranmer had that typical theologian's ability to weigh both sides of an issue. But the time comes for commitment. Cranmer put it this way with these words: "I have sinned, in that I signed with my hand what I did not believe with my heart. When the flames are lit, this hand shall be the first to burn." When the flames began, he leaned over and held his right hand in the fire until it was charred to a stump. Aside from this, he did not speak or move, except that once he raised his left hand to wipe the sweat from his forehead.

Many more illustrations of brave, highly educated men and women could be listed. Today, in the twenty-first century, we are told that as many men, women, and children are persecuted and murdered because of their loyalty to "this same Jesus" as at any time in the last 2,000 years. Don't you think that "this same Jesus" has clear, emphatic words to say to all those who follow Him in being senselessly murdered for His sake—even today?

---

7. W.C.B. "Notes and Queries, of Ridley, Latimer, Cranmer," *Oxford Journals*, Vols. 7-VIII, No. 104, p. 406; Wikipedia, articles on Ridley, Latimer, Cranmer, and Martyrs Memorial.

These earthly saints did not die for mere doctrine. They faced up to evil with joy in their hearts, because they knew their Lord through personal experience—that His example of joy under pressure was a joy that they understood, that His words of encouragement inscripted in the four Gospels were as true and living today as they were more than 2,000 years ago. "This same Jesus" was as real to them as He was to Paul under the axe and to Peter when He was crucified upside down.

In other words, He is just as real to you today. "This same Jesus" listens to every murmur for help and strength that any one of us can whisper. He is the same today as He was yesterday!

FOURTEEN

What Difference Does All This Make to Those Who Feel They Are Failures?

I add this chapter, because I know of many people, young and old, who believe they are failures. Some are parents who berate themselves for their prodigal sons and daughters—they feel they have done their best, but it wasn't good enough—especially parents who lose their children through suicide. Other parents know they could have done better. They see nothing but failure.

Middle-aged men and women, careful, diligent workers, suddenly find their companies downsizing, and thousands are given their pink slips. Many of them send out hundreds of résumés, and months go by with no interest—or "overqualified" is a frequent comment. They see and feel nothing but failure.

Others slip into foolish behavior and suddenly find themselves hooked on tobacco, alcohol, and drugs. They try to change, but they find their will power close to zero. They see nothing but failure.

Many young and old have been told by parents or other adults that they are "too slow," or, "not as pretty as their cousin," or, "too clumsy," or "a lousy student," or by a spouse, "you are a lousy lover," etc. So they live out these pathetic judgments that soon become self-fulfilling prophecies. They see nothing but failure.

What about all this human tragedy all around us? What can "this same

Jesus" say to us today about the shadow of failure that everybody who has ever lived has experienced some time, either long ago or this very moment?

Jesus and failure

Did Jesus experience failure? What would drive a consecrated, committed young man to cry out: "My God, My God, why have you forsaken Me" (Matthew 27:46)?

But this was not the first or only time Jesus felt "apparent failure."[1] Look again at John 1:11—"He came to His own, and His own did not receive him." That is, the very people He had chosen and been trying to empower did not recognize their own Leader! What could be sadder?

Think of the week that began with His triumphal entrance into Jerusalem. Jesus knew it would be His last. Think of His last visit to the Jerusalem temple, where He met only scowling, mean church leaders. Think of His last words to crowds around Him in a voice choking with anguish: "O Jerusalem, Jerusalem, the one who kills the prophets and stones those who are sent to her! How often I wanted to gather your children together, as a hen gathers her chicks under her wings, but you were not willing" (Matthew 23:37). In one sense, that is the cry of a failed mission! A "mysterious farewell" of a rejected Messiah!

Many heroic Christian leaders have gone to their death repeating similar, forlorn disappointment—their apparent failure.

What would Jesus say to us today, especially those who feel pressed down with a sense of failure, perceived or real? Of course, I cannot ignore Matthew 24:13—"He who endures to the end shall be saved." The Greek word translated as "endures" is the same Greek word translated as "patience" in Revelation 14:12—A more accurate translation would be, "Here is the endurance of saints."[2]

In other words, if one word describes those willing loyal who have lived through the terror of the end of the end time, "those who keep the commandments of God and the faith of Jesus"—it would be "endurance."

The key word that best describes Jesus throughout His ministry to the awful end at the Cross is *endurance.* "He who endures to the end shall be

---

1. Ellen G. White, *The Desire of Ages,* 678.

2. That Greek word translated either by "endurance" or "patience" is a combination word that describes a person who is able to carry a heavy load—a person who does not shirk, does not flinch. By the grace of God he carries the load of life—he does not quit, never gives up.

saved." My children often heard through the years, "We can always stand a little more. Never give up!" Whether it be pain, or disappointment, or even failure, I have watched them go through tough situations, and I believe they know how to endure.

I think often of the wisdom that President Theodore Roosevelt shared with the world, born of a lifetime of enduring when others said it couldn't be done:

> "It is not the critic who counts; not the man who points out how the strong man stumbles, or where the doer of deeds could have done better. The credit belongs to the man who is actually in the arena, whose face is marred by dust and sweat and blood; who strives valiantly; who errs and comes short again and again; who knows the great enthusiasms, the great devotions; who spends himself in a worthy cause; who, at the best, knows in the end the triumph of high achievement, and who, at the worst, if he fails, at least fails while daring greatly, so that his place shall never be with those timid souls who know neither victory nor defeat."[3]

I think of those two Australian physicians who, in April 1982, proposed that the bacterium called *Heliobacter pylori* was a common cause of ulcers. But even years later, according to the director of the Institute for Genome Research, Drs. Barry Marshall and Robbin Warren were "treated as village idiots." This discovery that bacteria caused stomach ulcers was one of the most amazing medical breakthroughs of this generation. This discovery was met with deafening silence from the medical community. But the most astounding response was from the pharmaceutical industry, which had more than eight billion dollars per year at risk in two drugs of choice, Tagamet and Zantac. For many years the medical world had blamed stress, coffee, spicy foods, or too much stomach acid for ulcers.

In the years following, medical research confirmed that over 90 percent of people with peptic ulcers were infected with the bacterium and that these infections could be eradicated by a one-week treatment with antibiotics and antibacterials. In fact, the treatment worked so well that the U.S. National Institutes of Health in 1994 issued an advisory to all American physicians to discontinue the prescription of Tagamet and Zantac for their ulcer patients.

Question: What would the world of suffering men, women, and children still be like if those two Australian physicians had not kept pressing their findings, in spite of the ridicule of their medical colleagues?

Winston Churchill gave the shortest commencement address ever given.

---

3. "Citizenship in a Republic" speech at the Sorbonne, Paris, April 23, 1910.

Though aging and sickly, he was asked to give the commencement address at Oxford University. He tottered to the podium. Hanging his cane on the desk, he peered at his young audience through his thick, bushy eyebrows, set his famous jaw, and exclaimed, "Never give up!"

He took a step back and again surveyed those eager young faces. Reaching into that great, inner reservoir of personal experience, Sir Winston's legendary voice rose in intensity, "Never give up!"

After an extra long pause, he roared, "Never give up!"

Then he took his cane and shuffled back to his seat. Stunned, the graduates sat in silence. Then the applause began, and ended in a thunderous, standing ovation for the old lion.

Sir Winston had delivered the briefest commencement address on record but perhaps the most memorable. It summed up his remarkable life: "Never give up!" If he had given up during the 1930s when most of his government colleagues had rejected him as irrelevant and a "has-been," we would never have heard the voice that most people say saved the free world in the 1940s.

If there is anything that I repeat more often to my grown-up children and their children, or to most any group I am asked to speak to, it is the simple plea, "Never give up!" I have watched many commendable projects begun with much enthusiasm, many energetic young salespersons, many passionate married couples, many excited students—but so many become discouraged "dropouts." They may even be ninety-day wonders—but watch out for Day 91!

Many are the examples of men and women who gave up too soon. I think of Willard Hershberger, catcher for the Cincinnati Reds. During an important baseball game, he signaled a wrong pitch. The batter hit a home run that cost the Reds the game. Hershberger worried about his mistake for days. He hardly spoke to anyone. He didn't smile; he paced the floor at night. No one could snap him out of his deepening depression.

On August 2, 1940, Hershberger did not come to the ballpark. He was found in his room, dead from his own hands—a no-hoper who thought himself a failure. He never knew of his Best Friend as his High Priest—he shut down the voice of the Holy Spirit who wanted him to see the big picture.

No one seems to understand the load you're carrying? Maybe, but don't give up! Jesus understands and knows exactly the encouragement you need.

You see no way out of the troubles at home? You may not, but Jesus, your High Priest does. Don't give up!

You feel as if you're working your socks off, and no one seems to recognize it? Perhaps, but don't give up!

You just learned that you have a sickness that may suddenly change all the plans for your future? Possibly, but don't give up! Jesus, at 33, knew about facing death too soon, and He knows what your tired mind needs to hear.

The Bamboo and the Fern

Perhaps our Lord wants us to hear the parable of the bamboo and the fern. A man who decided to quit his job, his relationships, even his religious commitments went to the woods to have one last talk with God. "God," he said, "Can you give me one good reason not to quit?"

God's answer surprised me. . . .

"Look around," He said. "Do you see the fern and the bamboo?"

"Yes," I replied.

"When I planted the fern and the bamboo seeds, I took very good care of them. I gave them light. I gave them water. The fern grew quickly. Its brilliant green covered the forest floor. Yet nothing came from the bamboo seeds. But I did not quit on the bamboo. In the second year, the fern grew more vibrant and plentiful.

"And again, nothing came from the bamboo seed. But I did not quit on the bamboo. In three years, there was nothing from the bamboo seed. But I would not quit. In year four, again, there was nothing from the bamboo seed. I would not quit!

"Then," He said, "in the fifth year a tiny sprout emerged from the earth. Compared to the fern, it was seemingly small and insignificant. But just six months later the bamboo rose to over 100 feet tall.

"It had spent the first years growing roots. Those roots made it strong and gave it what it needed to survive. I would not give any of my creations a challenger it could not handle."

Tenderly, He continued, "Did you know, my child, that all this time you have been struggling, you have actually been growing roots? I would not quit on the bamboo. I will never quit on you. Don't compare yourself to others."

Further, God said, "The bamboo had a different purpose than the fern.

Yet they both make the forest beautiful. Your time will come. You will rise high."

"How high should I rise?" I asked.

He asked in return, "How high will the bamboo rise?"

"As high as it can?" I questioned.

"Yes," He said, "Give Me glory by rising as high as you can."

Some days we feel wilted; other days, exultant. Let's remember that good days give us happiness; bad days give us experiences—both are essential to a successful life. Jesus knew both and can tell us how to handle both in our lives today.

Remarkable promises

I think of remarkably worded promises, such as:

"Whatever your anxieties and trials, spread out your case before the Lord. Your spirit will be braced for endurance. The way will be opened for you to disentangle yourself from embarrassment and difficulty. The weaker and more helpless you know yourself to be, the stronger will you become in His strength. The heavier your burdens, the more blessed the rest in casting them upon the Burden Bearer.[4]

"The Lord is disappointed when His people place a low estimate upon themselves. He desires His chosen heritage to value themselves according to the price He has placed upon them. . . . As Christ lived the law in humanity, so we may do if we will take hold of the Strong for strength. . . . Those who decide to do nothing in any line that will displease God, will know, after presenting their case before Him, just what course to pursue. And they will receive not only wisdom, but strength."[5]

'Worry is blind, and cannot discern the future; but Jesus sees the end from the beginning. In every difficulty He has His way prepared to bring relief. Our heavenly Father has a thousand ways to provide for us, of which we know nothing. Those who accept the one principle of making the service and honor of God supreme will find perplexities vanish, and a plain path before their feet."[6]

I remember the day when I took my children to Saratoga, in upstate New York. In 1777, the second Battle of Saratoga of the American Revolution gave the young Continental army one of its most decisive victories. I wanted my children to see a very interesting monument in the cemetery near the battlefield. The monument is dedicated to four generals of the

---

4. *The Desire of Ages*, 329.

5. ____, 668.

6. ____, 330

American Continental army who were in command of their groups during that remarkable colonial victory.

Benedict Arnold

General Gates was supreme commander for that day, they say, chiefly because of his political skill rather than his military merit. The battle for Saratoga would have been lost if Gates had not received the dashing heroism of Benedict Arnold at the right time. Reports say that Benedict Arnold late in the day did more with his 3,000 men than Gates did all day with his 11,000. Benedict Arnold was second only to Washington in the eyes of the Continental soldier.

But that monument! On that four-sided obelisk today, you will find the name and statue of Generals Gates, Schuyler, and Morgan. But on the fourth side, an empty niche remains for the hero of Saratoga. We pondered what might have been!

However, I especially wanted my children to see the second monument on the battlefield itself. Much, much smaller than the obelisk is a statue of a boot, the boot of Benedict Arnold. In the evening of the Battle of Saratoga, a wounded Hessian soldier, lying on the ground, fired at Arnold, shattering his left leg—that same leg that had been wounded in Quebec. A rifleman rushed upon the Hessian with drawn bayonet. He was stopped only by Arnold's cry: "For God's sake, don't hurt him!" It has been well said that that was the hour when the brilliant young general should have died.

A few months later, General Benedict Arnold, the commander of the fort at West Point, was plotting to turn the fort over to the British! By a chance coincidence, he was discovered, and he fled for his life to the British. The profit he received for his treason was a few thousand dollars and a commission in the British Army.

After becoming a Britisher, he asked an American prisoner, "What would the Americans do if they caught me?" With contempt, the American said: "They would cut off your wounded leg and give it the best of military burials—then, they would hang the rest of you."

Empty niche

So today there is an empty niche in Saratoga, New York. Benedict Arnold started well, but he didn't end well. Have you ever heard of a child named Benedict, or Judas, or Adolf? Everybody leaves some mark when they die. Happy memories for children to treasure; for others perhaps, great legacies of either worthy books or industries. Or prison records, or disappointed children for many reasons, or—a boot! How will you be remembered?

Jesus has given us all a sober warning: "He that endureth unto the end shall be saved!" We all can endure a little longer. "This same Jesus" would not make a promise to us that He Himself was not able honestly to experience. That is why when God tells all of us, "Never give up!"—He is not encouraging us to do the impossible. "The same Jesus" has been here where we now stand. He knows the bitter taste of "not succeeding"—where His own countrymen and, worse, His own closest friends, rejected Him. But He never gave up! Hanging on that awful cross, His breathing increasingly difficult, fever raging, and still time to climb down from that humiliating sideshow—but He chose to "endure the cross, despising the shame" (Hebrews 12:2), facing all that Evil could throw at Him, just for you and me. Though none of us has ever come close to such "failure," Jesus knows how close we may have come! Through it all, and perhaps for what is yet to come, Jesus knows exactly what kind of specific encouragement you need—and He can supply it. He knows the formula as to how to beat Satan at his own game. He is only a prayer away!

"This is the captain speaking."

I remember a speaking appointment in Corpus Christi, Texas, a few years ago. During some free time, my wife and I visited the *U.S.S. Lexington*, anchored in the harbor. It is the fifth ship in U.S. history to have that brave name. The fourth was lost in the Battle of the Coral Sea (May 1942) after a brilliant and heroic effort that stopped the advance of the Japanese toward Australia. As soon as this news hit America, the next aircraft carrier to be built was named the *Lexington*, which also soon saw gallant action in the Pacific.

On December 4, 1943, a Japanese bomber disabled this new *Lexington* on a moonlit night off Tarawa. The skipper, Captain Felix Stump, went to the ship speaker system so that all aboard could hear him: "This is the captain speaking. We have taken a torpedo hit in our stern, and the rudder seems badly damaged. *Each man must do his job calmly and efficiently. Don't worry. That's my job. I got you here and I'll get you out and home."* Marvelous story of how they limped home!

But there's more to the story. More than 95 percent of those on board had never been on the open sea before. They were not seasoned sailors and pilots. Citizen sailors and pilots, they were—recently assembled, trained, but unsure of themselves. On that moonlit night, they were an easy target, but the captain kept maneuvering the ship to face into the moonlight so that the *Lexington* would not give the bomber or submarine a broadside silhouette—all the while, changing his speed and direction.

On the way back to Pearl Harbor with that disabled rudder, the Admiral of the fleet radioed to Captain Stump, "That was wonderful seamanship, Captain." The Captain replied, "*Thank you, Sir, my crew was magnificent!*"

Those words swept through the crew: They were "magnificent" in the eyes of their captain! The sailors wrote home about their captain. When they limped back to Pearl, they didn't need the serenade of the Navy Band to make them feel as if they were heroes. They had already heard the commendation of their captain. Knowing their captain for what he was kept them unafraid, kept them doing their duty. They could trust their captain, because he got them there, and he would get them home.

One of these days, a wonderful group of people will, in a way, limp into the Harbor after the worst time of trouble ever to hit people on this earth—along with "an innumerable multitude" (Revelation 7:9) who also "endured unto the end." And they will hear their Captain say: "Well done, good and faithful servants. ... Enter into the joy of your lord" (Matthew 25:21).

And then He, "this same Jesus," who bears the scars of His own combat with Earth's powerful, malignant usurper, will turn to the unfallen worlds, to the unfallen angels, and wave His hand over the veterans from Earth, and say, "My crew was magnificent!"

Here are the people upon whom God risked His integrity and government. Here are the people since Calvary who threw their trust and loyalty on "this same Jesus," who led the way over and through "all the fiery darts of the wicked one" (Ephesians 6:16).

In a very special way, the rest of the universe that had been watching Laboratory Earth will stand and salute these veterans of a very costly war! And then these veterans turn to their Captain of the universe and fall on their knees in a sob that will echo from galaxy to galaxy—a sob of relief and gratitude and love! The risk was worth it! The Heavenly Trio can be trusted, and never again will the universe ever hear "No" again.

"This same Jesus," as our High Priest, fulfilled His role perfectly. Singing His praises as long as bluebirds fly and the Tree of Life yields fruit—that will be the joy of all intelligences throughout the universe.

FIFTEEN

What Difference Does All This Make to Those Who Believe in the Great Controversy?

One of the most overlooked appeals in our Lord's incredibly moving prayer to His Heavenly Father is recorded by John. You can look in hundreds of books and commentaries written by distinguished scholars, and scarcely a word recognizes the significant weight of John 17:18 and 20:21.

Before Jesus ascended, He laid out the job description for the Christian Church, speaking to His Father and ours: "As You have sent me into the world, I also have sent them into the world" (17:18; see also 20:21).

Obviously, this requires a second reading on our knees. Could He possibly mean what He said? *What Jesus was sent into this world to do, so He sends us to do!* Could it then be that, in some important aspects, the plan of salvation depends on His disciples' doing faithfully what He did so faithfully? And if they do not, they would be His followers in name only! And someday, such followers will hear those dreadful words, "I never knew you [for what you said you were]" (Matthew 7:23).

Heavenly Franchises

When I read this job description, I see God as our Heavenly Franchiser and Jesus as the Franchise's Prime Paradigm of what He expects out of His willing followers. Both God and Jesus have something special to offer everyone on Planet Earth who would "buy" from Him. He offers these franchises freely to all who will commit themselves to represent what He stands for—faithfully, clearly, day in and day out.

His marketing plan is to set up franchises worldwide—with everyone convinced that what He is selling is the most important enterprise in which anyone could invest.

Franchises in the normal business world are often taken back because local franchises did not live up to the name and expectations of head office. They did not faithfully reproduce the Master Pattern or the Master Recipe.

"This same Jesus" is the Divine Franchiser, who offers local franchises to men and women in every generation. He has had many takers. Some wanted His name but not His quality control. Some wanted His power but not His Spirit. Some wanted to capitalize on His advertising but not His character.

But Jesus has always found some, in every generation and in all lands, who get the point. They discovered that working for the Heavenly Franchise became their life! Nothing was more exciting! These local franchises know that they are not as perfect as is their Head Office. But they also know that if they would keep listening to Headquarters, especially to His omnipresent Spirit—the franchise's marvelous support system—their local franchise will increasingly reflect the original Pattern of the Divine Franchiser.[1]

At this point we must take a deep breath to remind ourselves of the Big Picture. We must remember that God made created intelligences on Planet Earth for a significant role in telling His side of the story in the controversy with Satan and his angels.

Why did He make "human beings . . . a new and distinct order"? *Because the human family would become one of His best laboratories for the working out of His "side" of the conflict, as well as providing an open display of how Satan's principles would work out.*

---

1. "When Christ left the world, He committed His work to His followers. He came to represent the character of God to the world, and we are left to represent Christ to the world."—*Signs of the Times*, April 15, 1889. "God designs that every one of us shall be perfect in Him, so that we may represent to the world the perfection of His character. He wants us to be set free from sin, that we shall not disappoint the heavenly intelligences, that we may not grieve our divine Redeemer. He does not desire us to profess Christianity and yet not avail ourselves of that grace which is able to make us perfect, that we may be found wanting in nothing, but unblamable before Him in love and holiness."—*Ibid.*, February 8, 1892. "In the exercise of his sovereign prerogative He imparted to His disciples the knowledge of the character of God, in order that they might communicate it to the world."— *Ibid.*, June 27, 1892

This "new and distinct order" of created intelligences was the "talk" of the universe: "All heaven took a deep and joyful interest in the creation of the world and of man. . . . They were made 'in the image of God' and it was the Creator's design that they should populate the earth."[2]

Further, the longer that men and woman (this "new and distinct order" of creation) would live, "the more fully [they] should reveal this image [Genesis 1:27]—the more fully reflect the glory of the Creator. . . . Throughout eternal ages he would have continued to gain new treasures of knowledge, to discover fresh springs of happiness, and to obtain clearer and yet clearer conceptions of the wisdom, the power, and the love of God. More and more fully would he have fulfilled the object of his creation, more and more fully have reflected the Creator's glory."[3]

God had great plans for the human race

Even further, God had planned that in the development of the human race He would "put it in our power, through co-operation with Him, to bring this scene of misery to an end."[4] That sounds like a lot of responsibility—the capacity to hasten the Advent (or delay it)!

Now, hours before Calvary and only a few weeks before His ascension, Jesus was putting Plan C into action. Plan A failed when Adam and Eve walked out of the Garden. Plan B failed when Israel missed its opportunity to be God's faithful franchise. Israel's privilege and mission, as God's "chosen people," was "to reveal the principles of His kingdom. . . . to represent the character of God. . . . He designed that the principles revealed through His people should be the means of restoring the moral image of God in man. . . . God withheld from them nothing favorable to the formation of character that would make them representatives of Himself. . . . God furnished them with every facility for becoming the greatest nation on the earth. . . . To all the world the gospel invitation was to be given. Through the teaching of the sacrificial service, Christ was to be uplifted before the nations. . . . As the numbers of Israel increased, they were to enlarge their borders, until their kingdom should embrace the world."[5]

Even after the Babylonian captivity Plan B was still workable—even in Christ's day! This is truly one more example of God's infinite patience: "If the leaders and teachers at Jerusalem had received the truth Christ

---

2. *Review and Herald*, February 11, 1902.

3. *Education*, 15.

4. *Ibid.*, 264.

5. *Christ's Object Lessons*, 285–290. See Isaiah 43:10, 12; 44:8.

brought, what a missionary center their city would have been! Backslidden Israel would have been converted. . . . How rapidly they could have carried the gospel to all parts of the world."[6] If Jerusalem's leaders "had heeded the light which Heaven had sent her, she might have stood forth in the pride of prosperity, the queen of kingdoms. . . . the mighty metropolis of the earth. . . . the world's diadem of glory."[7] God never gave up—Israel did![8]

Plan C

And then Plan C—the Christian church! Men and women of faith would become His divine franchises throughout the world, building the case that God can be trusted, that He is fair with His laws, that He is merciful beyond words, and that His grace melts our hearts and empowers weak wills so that His will can be done on earth even as it is done by joyful, enthusiastic, compliant angels in heaven (Luke 11:2). "That which God purposed to do for the world through Israel, the chosen nation, He will finally accomplish through His church on earth today."[9]

Surely the Christian church would get the point! "Don't make Israel's mistakes!" "Don't create a gap between belief and life!" "Learn the lessons of Israel!" So what happened?

In Plan C we have the same mission and purpose for the church that God had for Adam and Eve and for the Jewish nation: "Through His people Christ is to manifest His character and the principles of His kingdom. . . . He desires through His people to answer Satan's charges by showing the results of obedience to right principles."[10]

Plan C is a task not only for the corporate church. These "right principles," in contrast to satanic principles, "are to be manifest in the individual Christian. . . . All are to be symbols of what can be done for the world. They are to be types of the saving power of the truths of the gospel. All are agencies in the fulfillment of God's great purpose for the human race."[11]

---

6. *Ibid.*, 232.

7. *The Desire of Ages*, 576.

8. "This promise of blessing should have met fulfillment in large measure during the centuries following the return of the Israelites from the lands of their captivity. It was God's design that the whole earth be prepared for the first advent of Christ, even as today the way is preparing for His second coming."—*Prophets and Kings*, 703, 704. "Jerusalem would have stood forever, the elect of God."—*The Great Controversy*, 19.

9. *Prophets and Kings*, 713, 714.

10. *Christ Object Lessons*, 296.

11. *Ibid.*, 296, 297.

What specifically are these "right principles"? Christians, by definition, are to "possess the principles of the character of Christ."[12] Their appeal to the world will not be primarily in terms of denunciating "their idols, but by beholding something better. God's goodness is to be made known. 'Ye are My witnesses, saith the Lord, that I am God' Isa. 43:12."[13]

This connection between God's commission to the church—that the Christian's reflection of His character and principles would be His "witness" to the world, and that the return of Jesus depends on when this "witness" has been faithfully done—is neatly summarized in these words:

"It is the darkness of misapprehension of God that is enshrouding the world. Men are losing their knowledge of His character. It has been misunderstood and misinterpreted. At this time a message from God is to be proclaimed, a message illuminating in its influence and saving in its power. His character is to be made known. Into the darkness of the world is to be shed the light of His glory, the light of His goodness, mercy, and truth. . . . Those who wait for the Bridegroom's coming are to say to the people, 'Behold your God.' The last rays of merciful light, the last message of mercy to be given to the world, is a revelation of His character of love. The children of God are to manifest His glory. In their own life and character they are to reveal what the grace of God has done for them. The light of the Sun of Righteousness is to shine forth in good works—in words of truth and deeds of holiness."[14]

This is an amazing statement. Frankly, very unambiguous! It simply amplifies our Lord's prediction: "This gospel of the kingdom will be preached in all the world as a *witness* to all the nations, and then shall the end come" (Matthew 24:14).

Witnesses in any court do not repeat hearsay! They can speak only of what they personally know. God's faithful ones in the end-time will be personal witnesses to what the gospel has done for them and what it will surely do for all those who also "come and see."

Could it be said any clearer?

"All who receive Christ as a personal Saviour are to demonstrate the truth of the gospel and its saving power upon the life. God makes no requirement without making provision for its fulfillment. Through the grace of Christ we may accomplish everything that God requires. All the riches

---

12. *Ibid.*, 298.

13. *Ibid.*, 299.

14. *Ibid.*, 415, 416.

of heaven are to be revealed through God's people. 'Herein is My Father glorified,' Christ says, 'that ye bear much fruit; so shall ye be My disciples. John 15:8.'"[15]

These words are simple enough for a first-grader to understand. "This same Jesus" waits for His local franchises to do in their day what He did in His—glorify His Father in such a way that Satan's lies about God are exposed to the light of truth. And the promise is sure: the grace of power that made the babe of Bethlehem into the mighty revelation of God's character will be the same powerful grace that will transform willing men and women in the last generation into reproductions of "the same Jesus."

Basic Question

I know, the question is frequently asked: Why does Jesus need us as His plan C, to do for the world what Jesus did for thirty-three years? In other words, if Jesus beat Satan at every turn, if all heaven and unfallen worlds saw Satan unmasked when Jesus died,[16] why isn't the war over? If Jesus vindicated the character and government of God, what more is needed in order to end the great controversy? If Jesus settled everything in His life and death, why does God stand by and permit the horrors and sadnesses of the past 2,000 years? Was there something still unfinished after the cross?

Answers to these questions bring us back to why God created men and women as His "new and distinct order" in the universe. The human race was created to play an important role in the Great Controversy. They were not created to merely make Planet Earth more interesting. In some special way, men and women were to be the laboratory test of whose principles work best, God's or Satan's.[17]

In becoming a man "in every respect" (Hebrews 2:14, 17), Jesus led the way in shutting down Satan's accusations. But He also made it clear that more was yet to be done by those following His Example. He set up local franchises to continue doing throughout the world what He did for thirty-three years in a very limited area, east of the Mediterranean Sea.

What does this mean within the big picture? My favorite author sharpens our focus: "Satan was not then destroyed [at the cross]. The angels did not even then understand all that was involved in the great controversy. The principles at stake were to be more fully revealed. And for the sake of

---

15. *Ibid.*, 301.

16. When Jesus died on the cross, "Satan saw that his disguise was torn away."—*The Desire of Ages*, 761.

17. "Our little world is the lesson book of the universe."—*The Desire of Ages*, 19.

man, Satan's existence must be continued. Man as well as angels must see the contrast between the Prince of light and the prince of darkness. He must choose whom he will serve.[18]

Principles at Stake

What were some of those "principles" still "at stake"? Hard for us to believe today, but one of Satan's chief charges against God was that He was *basically self-centered*—that God was the Divine Paramour who wanted the adoration and submission of everyone, for selfish reasons.

We all have discovered that self-centered men and women still have difficulty appreciating genuine love—they think that what appears to be unalloyed, unselfish love must have a hook in it. Here Satan found some response in about one-third of the angels, because "from the beginning of the great controversy he has endeavored to prove God's principles of action to be selfish."[19] But our Creator's incarnation and sacrifice, a giving to humanity (John 3:16) that never gives up, proves Satan wrong, very wrong. Just watch Him die with your name on His mind!

To further justify his terrible charges, Satan pictured God (and still does) as "*severe and unforgiving*"—a "being whose chief attribute is *stern justice*—one who is a *severe judge, a harsh, exacting creditor.*" [20]

Satan takes delight in suggesting reasons why created intelligences should *mistrust God*, to "doubt His willingness and power to save us," that in some way, "the Lord will do us harm by His providences." He seeks to picture "the religious life as one of gloom. He desires it to appear toilsome and difficult; and when the Christian presents in his own life this view of religion, he is, through his unbelief, seconding the falsehood of Satan."[21]

---

18. *The Desire of Ages*, 761.

19. "Unselfishness, the principle of God's kingdom, is the principle that Satan hates; its very existence he denies. To disprove Satan's claim is the work of Christ and of all who bear His name."—*Education*, 154.

20. *Steps to Christ*, 10, 11. "Those whom he [Satan] had thus deceived imagined that God was hard and exacting. They regarded Him as watching to denounce and condemn, unwilling to receive the sinner so long as there was a legal excuse for not helping him."—*Prophets and Kings*, 311; see also *Testimonies*, vol. 5, 738. "Christ came to this earth to reveal the Father, to place Him in a correct light before men. Satan had aroused the enmity and prejudice of the race against God. He had pointed to Him as exacting, overbearing, and condemnatory, the author of suffering, misery, and death. He charged upon God the attributes of his own character."—*Manuscript Releases*, vol. 18, 331.

21. *Steps to Christ*, 116.

As one would expect, Satan included in his attack against God that God is *the author of sin, and suffering, and death.*[22] Imagine that! Would "this same Jesus" today visit a sick mother or banged-up teenager in the hospital and say, "Cheer up, it must be the will of God!" Heaven forbid!

Another one of "Satan's most successful devices to *cast reproach upon purity and truth*" has been his amazing skill in getting even Christians to misunderstand the nature of holiness. This surely must be one of his crowning deceptions: "Counterfeit holiness, spurious sanctification, is still doing its work of deception. Under various forms it exhibits the same spirit as in the days of Luther, diverting minds from the Scriptures, and leading men to follow their own feelings and impressions rather than to yield obedience to the law of God."[23]

Especially in our day, Satan's great skill is seen in how widespread the thought is that there are no absolutes, that everyone's opinion is as valid as anyone else's, that real liberty is found in "doing what's in your heart." That somehow there is a little divinity in everyone, and we should listen to each other.

As part of his charge that created beings did not really have freedom in view of God's magisterial appeal for his obedience, Satan simply charged that "*self-denial was impossible* with God and therefore not essential in the human family." Of course, Christ's life and death "broke forever the accusing power of Satan over the universe" on this and other accusations.[24]

Probably one of the most amazing charges Satan made against God's character and government has been echoing since humans began to ask questions: *If God were really fair and good, He would never have "permitted man to transgress His law"* and thus *"to sin, and bring in misery and death."* This "rebellious complaint against God" fails to understand that "to deprive man of the freedom of choice would be to rob him of his prerogative as an intelligent being, and make him a mere automaton."[25]

Another charge that Satan has succeeded in getting men and women—even professed Christians through the millennia—to accept is that *created beings can't keep the laws of* God. Thus, the Lawmaker was unfair in His dealings with created intelligences in threatening judgment on

---

22. *The Desire of Ages*, 24.

23. *The Great Controversy*, 193. Perhaps one of Satan's greatest achievements has been to redefine the gospel so that it is limited primarily to forgiveness.

24. *Selected Messages*, vol. 1, 341.

25. *The Desire of Ages*, 761.

commandment-breakers: "In the opening of the great controversy, Satan had declared that the law of God could not be obeyed, that justice was inconsistent with mercy, and that, should the law be broken, it would be impossible for the sinner to be pardoned."[26]

Misunderstanding God leads to many theological errors

Fritz Guy has clearly shown how misunderstanding the character of God has led to many theological errors: "One of the most serious ways in which the course of Christian theology has been misled by its classical and medieval heritage has been the assumption that the primary fact about God is omnipotent sovereignty and that the evidence of this sovereignty is the exercise of power to control events, including the actions of all of humanity. This assumption has kept a large part of the Christian tradition, both Catholic and Protestant, from hearing the gospel with clarity, because it has misunderstood the character of God."[27]

Summing up, these charges have become Satan's *modus operandi*, from the beginning of his subtle deceptions to this present day. The seed of evil has borne bitter fruit. Note the following recap:

"It is Satan's constant effort to misrepresent the character of God, the nature of sin, and the real issues at stake in the great controversy. His sophistry lessens the obligation of the divine law and gives men license to sin. At the same time he causes them to cherish false conceptions of God so that they regard Him with fear and hate rather than with love. The cruelty inherent in his own character is attributed to the Creator; it is embodied in systems of religion and expressed in modes of worship. Thus the minds of men are blinded, and Satan secures them as his agents to war against God. By perverted conceptions of the divine attributes, heathen nations were led to believe human sacrifices necessary to secure the favor of Deity; and horrible cruelties have been perpetrated under the various forms of idolatry."[28]

---

26. "Satan represents God's law of love as a law of selfishness. He declares that it is impossible for us to obey its precepts. The fall of our first parents, with all the woe that has resulted, he charges upon the Creator, leading men to look upon God as the author of sin, and suffering, and death."—The Desire of Ages, 24; see 117, 309. "Since the fall of Adam, men in every age have excused themselves for sinning, charging God with their sin, saying that they could not keep His commandments. This is the insinuation Satan cast at God in heaven."—Review and Herald, May 28, 1901.

27. Fritz Guy, "The Universality of God's Love," in *The Grace of God and the Will of Man*, ed., Clark H. Pinnock (Minneapolis, MN: Bethany House Publishers, 1989), 33. However, Pinnock and others work within the context that God has no knowledge of the immediate future because of man's freedom, etc.

28. "*The Great Controversy*, 569.

I know, this is all hard to believe—that a perfectly created angel, the first among all created intelligences, could ever think these thoughts. What is there about evil that makes it *so evil!*

Foot soldiers with cosmic significance

Philip Yancey captures one of the core truths of the Book of Job. Although He once wrote about Job's experience as "the Bible's most comprehensive look at the problem of pain and suffering," he later came to see the bigger picture:

"The contest posed between Satan and God is no trivial exercise. Satan's accusation that Job loves God only because 'you have put a hedge around him' stands as an attack on God's character. It implies that God is not worthy of love, in himself, that people follow God only because they get something out of it or are 'bribed' to do so. . . . The book hinges on the issue of integrity. Job acts as if God's integrity is on trial.

"The opening chapters of Job, however, reveal that God staked a lot on one man's wickedness or righteousness. Somehow, in a way the book only suggests and does not explain, one person's faith does make a difference. . . . Job reminds us that the small history of mankind on this earth—and, in fact, my own small history of faith—takes place within the larger drama of the history of the universe. We are foot soldiers in a spiritual battle with cosmic significance. . . . God's plan to reverse the Fall depends on the faith of those who follow him."[29]

Our Lord's divine franchises, representing the quality and spirit of the Home Office, became the arena where "the principles at stake were to be more fully revealed." In God's infinite wisdom, He put Himself at risk again when He gave to Christians the mission of completing the controversy between Him and Satan. The Christian church is God's Plan C "in the fulfillment of God's great purpose for the human race."[30]

Again, looking at the big picture, the Great Controversy theme explains why no one on earth would know what really happened on the cross *unless* "disciples" made it known. Would these "disciples" be believed if the "good news" they talked about did not make a difference in their lives, when compared with others who also had strong religious beliefs in their "gods"?

Paul was not "ashamed of the gospel of Christ"! Why not? Because

29. Philip Yancey, *The Bible Jesus Read* (Grand Rapids, MI: ZondervanPublishingHouse, 1999), 46 –67.

30. *Christ's Object Lessons*, 297.

everywhere the gospel was proclaimed, Paul and many others saw "the power [Lit: "dynamite"] of God" at work (Romans 1:16)!

Irrefutable evidence

What kind of power? He commended the Corinthians for choosing to make Jesus their Lord—Corinthians who once were "fornicators, idolaters, adulterers, homosexuals, sodomites, thieves, covetous, drunkards, revilers, and extortioners" (1 Cor.6:11). These early Christians began the long, glorious line of men and women who would present irrefutable evidence before Satan and all other doubters as to whether God can provide all that is needed to thwart evil whenever and however it shows itself.

Those early Christians were indeed "foot soldiers in a spiritual battle with cosmic significance."

If Satan with his accusations has put God on trial before the universe, then this human evidence proving God trustworthy must drive him furious—which is exactly what is happening (Rev. 12:17).

Paul looked forward to the day when Christians the world over and before the entire universe would make God look good—and Satan exceedingly furious:

"I am less than the least of all God's people; yet God gave me this privilege of taking to the Gentiles the Good News about the infinite riches of Christ, and of making all people see how God's secret plan is to be put into effect. God, who is the Creator of all things, kept his secret hidden through all the past ages, in order that at the present time, by means of the church, the angelic rulers and powers in the heavenly world might learn of his wisdom in all its different forms" (Ephesians 3:8–10, TEV; see also 1:4–12).[31]

God and the Church Both on Trial for the Same Reasons

God and the church are both on trial for the same reasons: to prove Satan wrong in all the charges and accusations that he has brought against the character and government of God. It could be argued, dear reader, that God needs you as much as you need Him, to get the Great Controversy settled!

---

31. "The point seems to be that the Lord is using us earthly benefactors of his cosmic victory (the church) to display to the angelic society of the heavenly realms, including the now defeated powers, the greatness of the Creator's wisdom in defeating his foes. We who used to be captives of the Satanic kingdom are now the very ones who proclaim its demise. The church is, as it were, God's eternal 'trophy case' of grace—we eternally exist 'to the praise of his glorious grace' (Ephesians 1:6, 12). —Gregory A. Boyd, *God At War* (Downers Grove, Ill: InterVarsity Press,1997), 252.

No wonder Ellen White was concerned enough to ask:

"In this crisis, where is the church to be found? Are its members meeting the claims of God? Are they fulfilling His commission, and representing His character to the world? Are they urging upon the attention of their fellowmen the last merciful message of warning?"[32]

Now the question: Is it possible that professed followers of Jesus Christ could ever be expected to help vindicate God in the great controversy? Everything we have said so far goes a long way toward answering that question. But let's linger at the implications that the question brings up. Would talk only about a crucified Jesus be any more than a history lesson, if "this 'same Jesus'" had not transformed the lives of the "talkers'?

Ezekiel in his day was concerned with this question and its answer. He was a captive with many other Israelites in Babylon; for hundreds of years, they had truly become an embarrassment to their Lord, and He could no longer defend them.

In referring to Plan B, God told Ezekiel how Israel had brought dishonor on His name and failed to fulfill their mission:

"But when they came to the nations, wherever they came, they profaned my holy name, in that men said of them, 'These are the people of the Lord, and yet they had to go out of his land.' But I had concern for my holy name, which the house of Israel caused to be profaned among the nations to which they came. Therefore . . . It is not for your sake, O house of Israel, that I am about to act, but for the sake of my holy name, which you have profaned among the nations. . . . And I will vindicate the holiness of my great name, which has been profaned among the nations. . . . and the nations will know that I am the Lord . . .when through you I vindicate my holiness before their eyes" (36:20-23, RSV).

How did God give Israel their last chance? He had been very patient

---

32. Ibid., 302. "It is God's purpose to manifest through His people the principles of His kingdom. That in life and character they may reveal these principles, He desires to separate them from the customs, habits, and practices of the world. . . . A great work is to be accomplished in setting before men the saving truths of the gospel. . . . To present these truths is the work of the third angel's message. The Lord designs that the presentation of this message shall be the highest, greatest work carried on in the world at this time. . . . The Lord designs through His people to answer Satan's charges by showing the result of obedience to right principles. . . .The purpose that God seeks to accomplish through His people today is the same that He desired to accomplish through Israel when He brought them forth out of Egypt. By beholding the goodness, the mercy, the justice, and the love of God revealed in the church, the world is to have a representation of His character. And when the law of God is thus exemplified in the life, even the world will recognize the superiority of those who love and fear and serve God above every other people on the earth."—*Testimonies*, vol. 5, 9-12.

with Israel, as He had with Lucifer in heaven. Even though the Israelite people were in captivity, they had not yet crossed the line; they still had time to learn from the mistakes of their fathers. So God beamed the light of hope on those exiles in Babylon; He would resurrect Plan B one more time.

This missing link that should have been recognized with great gratitude was Israel's need to see themselves as individual franchises, making clear and winsome the gracious appeal of their heavenly Father to men and women of all races and nationalities.

Those exiles heard the promise that God would "gather you from all the countries, and bring you into your own land." And now the conditions—it was a question of whether they wanted hearts of stone or of flesh: "A new heart I will give you, and a new spirit I will put within you; and I will take out of your flesh the heart of stone and give you a heart of flesh. And I will put my spirit within you, and cause you to walk in my statutes and be careful to observe my ordinances" (36:25–27, RSV)

Two Phases in Vindicating the Character of God

As we have seen, Plan B failed. God then initiated Plan C, His last plan, when He established the Christian church.

Our Lord's life and death were one phase of the vindication of God that lies at the heart of the Great Controversy. The second phase of vindicating the Name—the character—of God would be lived out through the work of grace in the lives of loyal Christians: "The Savior came to glorify the Father by the demonstration of His love; so the Spirit was to glorify Christ by revealing His grace to the world. The very image of God is to be reproduced in humanity. The honor of God, the honor of Christ, is involved in the perfection of the character of His people."[33]

The character of end-time Christians who "keep the commandments of God and the faith of Jesus" reflects the same quality exhibited in the lives of Enoch, Daniel, and all the others in times past who have let God give them new hearts and new spirits, hearts of flesh instead of hearts of stone.[34]

End-time Christians who have grasped the Lord's plan for His church will indeed grasp every day that they are important franchises, reflecting

---

33. *The Desire of Ages*, 761. "The honor of Christ must stand complete in the perfection of the character of His chosen people."—*Signs of the Times*, November 25, 1890.

34. "Enoch was a representative of those who will be upon the earth when Christ shall come, who will be translated to heaven without seeing death."—*Last Day Events*, 761.

the goals and purposes of the Head Office. Reproducing "the same Jesus" in all that they do is their highest joy.

Job understood all this, even before Jesus had come personally. Job's experience has been the template for faithful men and women ever since: "According to his faith, so was it unto Job. 'When He hath tried me,' he said, 'I shall come forth as gold.' Job 23:10. So it came to pass. By his patient endurance he vindicated his own character, and thus the character of Him whose representative he was."[35]

Christian's highest privilege

When we understand that the Christian's highest privilege is to join with Jesus in vindicating the character of God throughout the universe, our whole religious direction is turned upside down. Or is that right side up? Instead of focusing on self-centered reward and the need for constant approval, the deepest impulse becomes one of making the vindication of God, defending the goodness of God, supreme. Such is the gratitude of *agape* love in response to His magnificent love toward us.

J. B. Phillips said it well: "The responsibilities which faced Christ as a human being would be, if we stop to think, enough to drive the most balanced man out of his mind. But He maintained His poise, His joy and His peace. He did the Father's will; and that is both the most and the highest that we can do." [36]

When the clear outline of the issues in the Great Controversy is seen and brought home to the heart, the Pharisee's heart is transformed. He suddenly realizes that in truly doing God's will he could never find the joy of salvation in *external* religious behavior only.

In Luke 15, the elder brother, who probably had done "everything just right," is brought face to face with his father's love for his younger brother, perhaps understanding agape (love) for the first time—but he didn't know how to handle it.. When legalists are suddenly aware of what sin has cost God and how much they truly need His daily pardon and power, they are smothered in appreciation. Why? Before understanding the issues in the

---

35. *Education,*156. "It is God's purpose that His people shall be a sanctified, purified, holy people, communicating light to all around them. It is His purpose that, by exemplifying the truth in their lives, they shall be a praise in the earth. The grace of Christ is sufficient to bring this about. But let God's people remember that only as they believe and work out the principles of the gospel, can He make them a praise in the earth. . . . Not with tame, lifeless utterance is the message to be given, but with clear, decided, stirring utterances. . . . The world needs to see in Christians an evidence of the power of Christianity."—*Testimonies*, vol. 8, 14-16.

36. *Making Men Whole* (London: Fontana Books, 1952), 79.

Great Controversy, the Pharisee, the elder brother, the legalist, had been "working, not from love, but from hope of reward."[37] They each were doing their "duty," not to honor God or their father, but to impress Him!

When Plan C is understood within the purposes of the Great Controversy, it embraces all aspects of the Christian's life. Everything takes on a new color; a new kind of breeze is blowing. A new reason for everything we do becomes clear and motivating. Ellen White's plea echoes throughout her writings:

"If there was ever a people in need of constantly increasing light from heaven, it is the people that, in this time of peril, God has called to be the depositaries of His holy law, and to vindicate His character before the world. Those to whom has been committed a trust so sacred must be spiritualized, elevated, vitalized, by the truths they profess to believe."[38]

Further, "It becomes every child of God to vindicate His character. You can magnify the Lord; you can show the power of sustaining grace."[39] Truly, it is simply reproducing in our limited way "this same Jesus," in the same way that Jesus vindicated the character of God.

Would any Christian who understands what Jesus did in the Garden and on the Cross want to do any less? Those who understand how much God needs their witness are on the way to fulfilling God's Plan C.

Yancey finds enormous significance in the cosmic wager between God and Satan as revealed in the Book of Job. He sees the same "wager" being played out "in other believers as well. We are God's Exhibit A, his demonstration piece to the powers in the unseen world. . . .The New Testament insists that what happens among us here will, in fact, help determine the future of that universe. Paul is emphatic: 'The whole creation is on tiptoe to see the wonderful sight of the sons of God coming into their own.' [Romans 8:19, Phillips]. . . . God has granted to ordinary men and women the

---

37. *Christ's Object Lessons*, 209. Even the disciples had difficulty getting all this straight. "While they had been attracted by the love of Jesus, the disciples were not wholly free from Pharisaism. They still worked with the thought of meriting a reward in proportion to their labor. They cherished a spirit of self-exaltation and self-complacency, and made comparisons among themselves . . . He would not have us eager for rewards, nor feel that for every duty we must receive compensation. We should not be so anxious to gain the reward as to do what is right, irrespective of all gain. Love to God and to our fellowmen should be our motive."—*Christ's Object Lessons*, 396-399.

38. *Testimonies*, vol. 5, 746.

39. *Ibid.*, 317. "Like our Savior, we are in this world to do service for God. We are here to become like God in character, and by a life of service to reveal Him to the world. In order to be coworkers with God, in order to become like Him, and to reveal His character, we must know Him aright."—*The Ministry of Healing*, p. 409.

dignity of participating in the Great Reversal which will restore the cosmos to its pristine state."[40]

Honoring God rather than impressing Him

Vindicating the character of God cannot be done with a religious posture that aims at *impressing* God with good deeds—even with faithful tithing and Sabbath observance. Vindicating and reflecting the character of God involve *honoring* God in tithing and Sabbath hours—the difference between "the yoke of bondage" (Galatians 5:1) and the joy of commitment.

For centuries, the armies of earth have had their flags that became their center, their inspiration to do what seemed impossible. "It's striking how often flags are mentioned in the [Congressional] Medal of Honor citations for the Civil War. Out of 1,520 Medal of Honor actions during the Civil War, 467 were given to men who either defended the flag of their side or captured a flag of the Confederate."[41]

The flag-bearer was at the center of the storm of battle, the most vulnerable. Although he carried no weapons, he was always at the head of the charge. Soldiers always kept one eye on his flag, because it told them if their group was advancing or retreating. And, of course, the enemy kept their eye on that flag too. They knew that bringing down the flag-bearer was the quickest way to disrupt the attack. The command, "Rally 'round the flag" was not merely a romantic phrase—it meant the difference between success and failure for the regiment.

Few held the flag throughout the war; too many fell. But one, Leopold Karpeles of the 46th (later the 57th Massachusetts Volunteer Regiment) volunteered to be the color-bearer in 1862 and was invalided on July 30, 1864—too wounded to continue. Leaving Prague when he was eleven, he was forever grateful for his newfound freedom in America. This gratitude gave him the motivation to pay back what he owed to his new homeland. His exploits in the various battles, beginning with the Goldsboro Expedition and through the Battle of the Wilderness, Spotsylvania, and the Battle of the Crater—became legendary. His commanders were in awe with his courage, always exposing himself to the blizzard of lead in order to make the flag more visible.

His CMH citation included these words: "While color bearer, rallied the retreating troops and induced them to check the enemy's advance . . ."

---

40. Philip Yancey, *Disappointment With God* (Grand Rapids, MI: Zondervan Publishing House, 1988), 170-173.

41. Allen Mikaelian, *Medal of Honor* (New York: Hyperion, 2002), 19.

Throughout human history, God has had His color-bearers, His flag-bearers. Many known; many more unknown. When we think of Joseph, Moses, Joshua, Elijah, Daniel, and Paul, our hearts skip a beat. Somewhere in God's universe, something even more meaningful than the CMH will be given to their kind—even today men and women are rallying 'round the flag' because, with their courage and loyalty to "this same Jesus," they desire to do nothing that would bring dishonor to the flag of truth and His Holy Name

In the end time, God's last-day loyalists will raise the flag in the face of its enemies. Honest men and women the world over will eventually rally "round the flag" represented by the seventh-day Sabbath. It will take all the perseverance, courage, and quiet loyalty of Leopold Karpela for God's loyalists to face latter-day blizzards, not of soft lead, but of ridicule, disdain, or material hardship.

This Sabbath flag represents the honor of God in the Great Controversy. It is surely under attack wherever one looks these days. But God has given His flag to men and women who claim His name. They will be the color-bearers in the last scene in the great drama, when the curtain is about to come down. They will have a message so compelling that honest men and women around the world will "step out from the rebel flag" and stand under freedom's flag—"the blood-stained banner of Prince Emmanuel."[42]

Sounds like a lot of responsibility to be dumped on frail men and women, even though they call themselves Christians. So we ask, how can weak human beings ever be expected to "vindicate" the character of God, to be faithful franchises, reflecting the quality and message of "this same Jesus"? How can we carry His flag so that He will not be embarrassed? How will we become safe even to receive the flag?

We do it by "faith"—that great New Testament word that describes the willing commandment keeper devoted to every living word that has come out of the mouth of "this same Jesus," whether it is found in the Bible or in the quiet whispers of the Holy Spirit. John the Revelator said it best: those in the last generation who "keep the commandments of God and the faith of Jesus" (Revelation 14:12) are loyal commandment keepers, because "this same Jesus" gives to them the keeping power that kept "this same Jesus" faithful 2,000 years ago!

---

42. *Review and Herald,* July 7, 1904.

SIXTEEN

How Long Will Jesus Remain As Our High Priest?

Low long "this same Jesus" will remain as our "all-mighty Mediator"[1] in the Most Holy Place in the heavenly sanctuary is *easy to answer*! His work is over when all living on Planet Earth in the end time have made up their minds as to whether they have submitted themselves to truth, as the Holy Spirit has revealed it to their conscience (Romans 2:15, 16)—or have instead become settled into resisting the Holy Spirit. Some, obviously, will have more truth than others, but all will have enough truth to make long-lasting decisions.

Sometime soon these fateful words will be said: "Let the evildoers still do evil, and the filthy still be filthy, and the righteous still do right, and the holy still be holy" (Revelation 22:11, RSV). The Revelator depicts the end of our Lord's mediatorial work as decision time, when all have finally chosen either to receive the seal of God of the mark of the beast (Revelation 7:2, 3; 13:17).

God does not want evil to continue one day longer than necessary. He has longed to intervene and end all war, all crime, and all suffering. Of course, He can do it swiftly and fairly. But in this Great Controversy with Satan, God has put Himself on the line, with His honor at stake throughout the universe. In some way we will understand more clearly in the future, but in God's great plan, the jury is still out! Why? Some final events in the Great Controversy have yet to be played out.

1.   Ellen G. White, *The Great Controversy*, 488.

Rebels will not live forever

God has made it clear that rebels will not inherit the New Earth. The unfallen universe does not want to see selfish, power-hungry, coercive people living forever. That kind of self-centered mischief started the universe-wide controversy in the first place! The universe will know, with the evidence before all to see, when God has decided that His "purpose to place things on an eternal basis of security" has been fulfilled.[2]

What is God's open plan? Our Lord's solution is to give men and women, in all times and places, all the resources necessary to withstand the Evil One, to overcome "as I also overcame" (Revelation 3:21). *Those who overcome can be trusted with eternal life!*

How will we know when that final showdown will happen? Have we been told what God is looking for before He blows the final whistle that the game is over?

Revelation 7 tells us that God (yes, God!) is holding back the terror of the seven last plagues. Revelation's seven last plagues are on hold! Why? Because He is waiting for people whom He can seal! The forces of evil are restrained "till we have sealed the servants of our God on their foreheads. And I heard the number of those sealed, One hundred and forty-four thousand . . . sealed" (Revelation 7:3).

When Jesus will return

This text tells us when Jesus will return! Revelation 14 picks up this story where John, in vision, sees this symbolic group of 144,000 "who had his name [the Lamb's; that is, Christ] and his Father's name written on their foreheads." In John's vision of Revelation 22, he sees those who surrounded the throne of God: "They shall see his face, and his name shall be on their foreheads."

They have learned one of the secrets of our Lord's Prayer: "Hallowed be Thy Name."

What a wonderful future for those who "follow the Lamb wherever he goes. . . .and in their mouth no lie was found, for they are spotless" (Revelation 14:4). They can be trusted with eternal life!

But what does John mean that the time of the end is being stretched out until God can seal people with His signature of approval?

What on earth could John be describing? Why is God holding back

---

2. ____, *The Desire of Ages*, 759.

these last-day winds of terror and destruction? Why is He telling angels to "Hold, hold—hold back the north wind of nuclear war. South wind—hold back those seven last plagues!" Why? "God's people are not ready! Hold back the east wind of human madness!" Why? "God's people haven't caught on yet as to the purpose of the gospel!" "Hold back the west wind of satanic fury, until God's people are ready to carry out their last assignment. Hold the winds until God's people are ready to be sealed. Hold the winds until His people are ready for His stamp of approval. Hold the winds until His people are ready for God to use them in His final message to earth's last generation—people who will not embarrass Him."

How many more years?

How many more years must God keep holding these winds? We know on good authority that He never intended to hold them this long! How many more years must Jesus remain as our "all-powerful Mediator"? John is telling us with divine precision—when end-time people have shown the universe whether they are mature "wheat" or mature tares!

What will identify God's people in these last days? Sabbath-keeping, health-reforming tithe-payers? Yes and No! After all, Sabbath-keeping, health-reforming, tithe payers once crucified God!

John tells us how God's people will be identified in the last days—they will have the Father's name written on their foreheads. They will be sealed with His approval. Many products can't be sold without a certain seal of approval. Those seals tell the world that the product has passed all the tests—such as that little yellow seal of the Underwriter's Lab on the bottom of electrical appliances or imprinted in the plastic casing.

What's the importance of a seal? Every gasoline pump has one. In other words, we can trust the pump that we will get the exact amount of gasoline for which we're paying! The same for elevators. No seal—no service! What's the value of a signature? Ask any art collector, or clock collector, ask any world-class violinist as he checks his Stradivarius. Why do people buy Tiger Wood golf clubs or Venus Williams tennis rackets? Or look for Ralph Lauren shirts and Tommy Hilfiger sweaters, or buy Gucci or Dooley Bourke handbags or shoes? Or those looking for a reliable washing machine (perhaps a Maytag or Kenmore)—or a lawn mower (maybe a Craftsman or Toro).

For most products, the name means everything. It means that the product carries the endorsement of someone who cares about quality, someone who can be trusted—therefore you can trust those Tiger Woods golf clubs or a Kenmore washer (best quality, according to *Consumer Reports*). Those names mean quality, and you can trust anything that those names are on.

Remember those TV ads for Hanes clothing? Can't you see that determined female inspector on the assembly line, with all of her formidable charm, looking over each item: "They don't say Hanes until *I* say they say Hanes!"

Quality goes in before the name goes on

Down here in these days of the held winds, that is what God is telling the universe when He writes His name in the foreheads of His willing faithful: "Listen to them," He is saying, "You can trust what they say. I am proud to give them my seal of approval. *The quality goes in before My name goes on.*"

What could be more wonderful than to have our heavenly Father write His name across our forehead? Is this a group we want to be a part of, or what? With that signature, God is saying, "Here are people who have let my Holy Spirit do His work—people who indeed are telling the truth about Me. I am not embarrassed by how they represent Me, and they have my seal of approval."

The Bible calls this process of having God's signature on our lives, the "sealing work." And this is what all heaven is focusing on today. And that is why Jesus still waits. Satan knows it, God knows it. Do we?

This is why Jesus remains in the Most Holy Place in the heavenly sanctuary today! He is still working with the willing, He wants them so settled into the truth that they will never be moved to say "No" to God, ever again. They will be so settled into the truth that their habits of mind and body will be as predictable, as natural, as habitual as blinking their eyes.[3] Habitants of unfallen worlds can trust them! Angels can trust them! The whole universe will endorse God's judgments—that these willing loyalists from Earth are safe to be given eternal life.

Not long from now the whole universe—unfallen worlds, angels, and the redeemed of earth—will sing in a mighty choir: "Hallelujah! Salvation and glory and power belong to our God, for his judgments are true and just" (Revelation 19:1, 2).

Cut short the work

---

3. "Just as soon as the people of God are sealed in their foreheads—it is not any seal or mark that can be seen but a settling into the truth, both intellectually and spiritually, so they cannot be moved—just as soon as God's people are sealed and prepared for the shaking, it will come. Indeed, it has begun already."—*Last Day Events*, 219, 220.

Jesus finally has His willing loyalists, through whom He can "finish the work and cut it short in righteousness" (Romans 9:28). He will cut His work short when He has people that He can trust with His power—"latter rain" power. God is waiting for people whom He can empower without embarrassing His Name.

One of these days our High Priest will become the Groom—a Groom who has waited long at the altar for His bride to "make herself ready" (Revelation 19:7). And then what a marvelous wedding reception we will behold!

A long table will be set with the best of silver and far better than Blue Willow or Wedgewood china. In a way, a name card will be placed at each plate. Your name is on one of those name cards. You can be sure that there will be fathers and mothers going up and down that long table looking for a son or daughter. Or children looking for their parents. Or a wife looking for her husband—a husband looking for his wife. But there will be empty seats at that table.

The real question today, the only one with any lasting significance, should be: Will you and I be in our places, singing out what we have found to be true—that God has been super faithful, that He can be trusted, and that you and I will serve Him forever?

Let Him help us get ready for the great wedding reception. He will do all that is necessary to help us get dressed in the proper wedding clothes—"in fine linen, clean and bright, for the fine linen is the righteous acts of the saints" (Revelation 19:8). However, I have never heard of a bridegroom dressing his wife for their wedding! Some things a groom doesn't do, or can't! In the wedding of all weddings, the Bridegroom does His part—He provides the wedding clothes. But He must wait for His bride, you and me, to put on the wedding garment!

But He will help us all He can as we joyfully, finally, get ourselves ready. He will help us get ready to be *safe to save,* for that is His job as our Saviour! And that is His promise to all of us in Revelation 19.